THE INTEGRATED SELF

Your Guide to Authentic Personal and Spiritual Growth

Patrick Diorio and Arianna Sidway

ISBN 979-8-89112-487-5 (Paperback)
ISBN 979-8-89309-201-1 (Hardcover)
ISBN 979-8-89112-488-2 (Digital)

First Edition

Covenant Books
11661 Hwy 707
Murrells Inlet, SC 29576
www.covenantbooks.com

CONTENTS

PREFACE

This book is offered in the spirit of openness, understanding, acceptance, inclusion, kindness, and love. We ask you to suspend your prejudices, opinions, and criticisms that create a divide between the differing belief systems in the world, and that are especially amplified by the debates taking place in the online world.

In particular, there is an intense emotional connection to the specific words that we use to describe our relationships to the spiritual realm of existence. There seems to be a reluctance, even a resistance to acknowledge the possible validity of other beliefs, or to even allow others to hold differing or opposing beliefs.

Why does it really matter whether someone refers to their creator as God, Creator, Source, Spirit, the Universe, the Divine, Yahweh, Jehovah, the list goes on, and is practically endless nowadays? We suspect that we argue the specific name used for "God," so we do not come close to validating the corresponding or opposing belief systems. Maybe we outright reject the specific names others use for "God" in an effort to validate our own respective belief systems.

What if we are all right? What if everyone's varied belief systems, each and every variation were actually and literally valid? What if the universal rule of existence in this world, whether you are living in the 3D, 4D, or 5D world, or a combination, literally is: If you believe it, it is so. What if you believe without a doubt, you then actually see it, hear it, touch it, feel it, and experience it?

On the contrary, what if we are all wrong? What if no one's belief system is accurate, maybe not even close to being accurate? What if the feeling of needing to know is actually one of the distractions or misdirections of the "matrix" to keep us stuck, confused, or so sure of our own belief system that we stop considering the truth of it all; that we are all connected and that the actual truth would destroy the very existence of the matrix if we could all come together under the blanket of understanding, kindness, compassion, light, and love.

At the time of this book being written, there are a lot of debates and divisions on the internet shaming those who may not agree with our respective beliefs. After discussing, we feel that it is pointless to argue and convince others to believe our beliefs, and also that in the eyes of God (or whoever your Creator is), this very arguing and division is the opposite of what God would want. It is our ultimate belief and goal to encourage everyone to find a path and belief system that feels true to you, even if it happens to not be ours. We welcome all, no matter what your beliefs may be, or come to be. We believe the ultimate goal is for every single person to have a belief system unique to them or find one that resonates deeply in your soul.

While this book includes and acknowledges mental health and healing in regard to your spiritual practice, please know that our goal is for you to find a belief system that feels aligned with you, specifically. Arianna, for example, has hopped around a few different belief systems before creating her own spiritual practice, extracting ideas and beliefs from many areas. She realized there wasn't a box with a label already existing that fit her beliefs and created her own by connecting to the Divine. On the other hand, if you do practice a particular religion or have your words and lingo to describe your creator, that is amazing. We welcome everyone in this book and hold space for you here to be your authentic self and use your belief system where fit.

In this spirit, and for the purposes of consistency, we ask for your indulgence and allow us to use the words God, Spirit, Source, The Universe, and The Divine, interchangeably with respect, in the intended spirit of inclusion of all beliefs. Simply insert your personal/preferred verbiage where these terms lie to have an experience that matches your beliefs while you read this book.

PART 1

The Journey to Balanced Growth and Inner Peace

Section 1.1—We're Going on an Adventure, Are You Along for the Ride?

As a spiritual being having your own unique human experience, you are under no obligation to explain yourself or your life's journey to anyone. You do not owe the world an explanation of your life, your path, your purpose, or your story. It is not your responsibility to help people understand who you are and help them to be comfortable with your life choices. However, you do owe it to yourself to become aware of your own personal ego and subconscious mind, and the role they play in the choices you make and the path you take. Once you are aware of all aspects of Self, the choice of experiences is consciously and powerfully yours.

Are you aware, fully conscious, and in control of your own actions and reactions to your physical environment that is filled with opportunities for you to be provoked and triggered, while also filled with lessons to be learned and growth to be realized?; or are you an unconscious puppet being directed through life by the pulls and tugs on your strings by your subconscious puppeteer? Are you the unwitting main character in someone else's story, motivated by programmed actions and reactions from the perspective of a wounded inner child? Are you the antihero in your own melodramatic movie based on a traumatic childhood, a series of seemingly wrong choices, and an unfortunate sequence of life events? Are you sleepwalking through life as the victim in a dream state, feeling lost in the fog of a hopeless situation?

It is now time for you to cut the strings, and to awaken to your own reality. It is time for you to be a real-life superhero in your own real-world adventure, pitting yourself against great obstacles and challenges that only you would be able to bravely face, fiercely battle, and ultimately defeat, overcoming great odds. Now is the time for you to become aware of the pieces and parts of your Self, your authentic Self; the parts of you that make up who you really are in your mind and soul, to become conscious of the true essence of you and embrace them lovingly and compassionately.

This is your nudge and a wake-up call for you to stop hitting the snooze button on your alarm clock, to wake up to a new day, a new mindset, to a renewed sense of being, potentiality, and the possibility of a new life trajectory. Today is the dawn of a new day, when you finally begin to live consciously, courageously, and committed to a life of awareness, conscious choices, balanced growth, and expanded consciousness. Today is the day that you stop living to someone else's expectations and start living a life of conscious choice and self-determination without the guilt of putting yourself first, without apology to anyone, or the approval of others. Today you become consciously aware that your authentic Self lies within, ready to step into the light and finally live in a pure expression of your authenticity.

How do we get to know our authentic selves, and what does that mean? In the Integrated Self Model (the Model), it means that you are aware, conscious, and evolving. It does not mean that you have it all together and under control, not necessarily balanced and integrated yet. Being your authentic self means that you embrace all that you are without the masks and filters that you have been unconsciously wearing from your early childhood from all of the pain and trauma that you have experienced. By embodying your authentic Self, you accept the good and bad, the light and dark, the divine and shadow aspects of all that you are.

While you must move through the painful memories of the past in order to become your authentic Self, we caution you to…

> be prepared; you can't know what memories will be triggered as you reacquaint yourself with the (child) you were once upon a time. But remember, you're not alone. Your Authentic Self is with you, a loving spiritual companion ready to help unravel the tangled threads of memory, promise, and abandonment… Pain is part of the past. There isn't one of us who doesn't still carry childhood wounds… With patience and quiet observation, these events will provide your authentic archaeologist with a continuous source of information] that will reassuringly lead you back to your Self.[1]

Ask yourself, what is it that you want to be doing? Who do you want to be? What brings you joy? What will allow you to connect the dots between who you are now and who you are to become? What can you be doing in the here and now in order for you to uncover and experience your authentic Self? These are the questions that you will need to fully embrace and honestly answer if you are to find contentment, purpose, passion, and peace in this lifetime. You must come to understand where you are in your journey in order to have a meaningful human-spirit experience. The choice of experience is yours, and please come to know that there are no wrong choices or wrong decisions, but instead different experiences. That is, there is no wrong choice if you are consciously assessing the pros and cons, including the possible outcomes and consequences for yourself as well as for others.

The role of choice is one of the foundational pillars of the Integrated Self Model and is crucial to its validity. For us, there is no doubt that life is a series of choices and we define ourselves by the choices we make. The difference that conscious choice will have on the quality and trajectory of our lives is huge,

> Our choices can be conscious or unconscious. Conscious choice is creative, the heart of authenticity. Unconscious choice is destructive, the heel of self-abuse. Unconscious choice is how we end up living other people's lives... We live in a world defined by duality—light or dark, up or down, success or failure, right or wrong, pain or joy. This duality keeps us in perpetual motion. Like a pendulum in an old clock, we swing back and forth through our emotions. But creative, conscious choice gives us the power to stop swinging and remain in balance, at peace.[2]

> The center of the evolutionary process is choice. It is the engine of your evolution. Each choice that you make is a choice of intention... You cannot choose your intentions consciously until you become conscious of each of the different aspects of yourself... Each of these aspects has its own values and goals. If you are not conscious of all of the different parts of yourself, the part of yourself that is the strongest will win out over the other parts... The choice of intention is also the choice of karmic path... Conscious evolution through responsible choice is the accelerated way of evolution... Responsible choice is the conscious road to authentic empowerment... The choice not to choose is the choice to remain unconscious... Responsible choice is a choice that takes into account the consequences of your choices... Only through responsible choice can you choose consciously to cultivate and nourish the needs of your soul, and to challenge and

> release the wants of your [ego]. This is the choice of clarity and wisdom, the choice of conscious transformation… It is the choice to follow the voice of your higher self, your soul… It is the path that leads consciously to authentic power.[3]

This is the path that leads consciously to your Authentic Self.

In addition to choice, balance and integration are the other essential elements of the Integrated Self Model. These concepts may be new to you as they directly relate to ego development and soul evolution, or perhaps you've heard these terms before in relation to healing and spirituality. It has long been held as the norm for the ego and soul to be mutually exclusive of each other. It was (and still is) believed by many that a person could either be only of a very human, ego-based existence, strongly focused on the material aspects of the world, or a person could only be spiritually evolved, requiring that the ego mind be quieted or suppressed. It is common to believe that the ego must die in order for true spirituality to flourish. We may hear the words *ego death* in certain spaces, which leads to the insinuation that the ego must be discarded or thrown out. The essence of the Integrated Self Model is that yes, the ego might have to crumble and be reconstructed (i.e., ego death); however, the ego does provide valuable insight and needs to be integrated into the Self, instead of thrown out and not paid attention to. The Integrated Self Model shows how the ego is formed and may need to be reformed as our beliefs change and as our soul awakens, so that both the ego and soul can be integrated to create your Self-identity.

When examining the Integrated Self Model, you will see that the two seemingly opposed and competing sides are the ego development process and the soul evolution process. At certain parts of your journey, it may truly feel as though these two sides of Self oppose each other. The goal is to create a respectful and harmonious relationship between the ego and soul, each with its own job and purpose. The ego is to be responsible for the doing, planning, and action steps (the human stuff), and the soul is to be responsible for being, experiencing, and exploring (the spiritual stuff). Therefore, according to the Model, the quality of the human-spirit experience is the direct result of the relationship formed between the ego and the soul. The more out of balance that the ego and soul are in terms of growth and integration, the more internal confusion, stress, and difficulty you will experience. The more both sides are balanced and integrated, the more that consciousness will expand, and the more contentment and peace you will have.

The balance of the ego and soul is the very essence of the Integrated Self Model. When you are focused on only one aspect of your Self (ego development or soul evolution), you are acting in a one-dimensional manner, ignoring the aspects of the other, which creates an imbalance that brings more confusion, stress, anxiety, depression, physical illness, the list goes on. The more that your ego and soul are out of balance, the greater the mental and emotional symptoms experienced. When you fail to create a complementary relationship between your ego and your soul, you do not give your Self the time or the chance to integrate with the whole of your identity and will find your Self fluctuating between feeling that you are spiritually at peace and feeling that you have regressed back into your old ego-based habits to be self-sabotaging or self-destructive in nature. At the very least, you are not in alignment with your choices, plan, purpose, and path for encompassing all that you are on the way to becoming your authentic Self.

The ego development process and the soul evolution process basically follow the same high-level repeated steps. These steps include observing, learning, understanding, choosing, changing, and experiencing. They differ only in that each has its own goals and interests. The ego is interested in the human aspects of living in this physical world, keeping us safe while doing our best among the other doers in the world. The ego has long been equated with personal identity; however, as you will see in the Model, this is only half the story and most of the reason why human beings struggle so much. Once the soul is working in harmony with the ego, the soul remains focused on our connection and relationship to Source, and the Ego gains a strong ally for being, as well as doing, in the 3D world.

Inspirational Author and Speaker Caroline Myss emphasizes the importance of our Soul in our human-spirit journey,

> We ignore our soul to our peril. And today we ignore the existence of the human soul, as if it were no more than a religious object or a deeper psychological term. But the soul is the power battery of the human life and all that a person's life includes. I know that now. The strength of the soul is pure titanium. And the wounds of our soul can shatter us for the whole of our life. We stand little chance of becoming a whole person when we dismiss the existence or power of the soul... I believe we are meant to understand our mind-body as individual spiritual powers expressive of a greater Divine energy. We are meant to discover both our personal power and our shared purpose for being alive within a spiritual context.[4]

> When you resonate at the soul level, at your soul's essence, you attract soul mates and soul experiences down here on earth. When you just decide to only resonate at the human level, you attract lessons. So how do you clear up the lessons? You get connected, connect to your soul and integrate it into your human experience... and watch your life completely change.[5]

On the other hand, if you decide to resonate only at the soul level, rejecting your Ego and focusing only on the spiritual aspect of your Self-identity, you become more and more detached from the physical world and increase the likelihood of experiencing physical and mental health issues.

As discussed later, your Self-identity is composed of both your Ego identity and your Soul identity. This Model stresses that in all things related to your ego and soul, both are good, balance is better, and the Integrated Self is best. As evidence of our own respective journeys through the development of the ego with choice and change, the spiritual awakenings, the soul's evolution, the deliberate integration of ego and soul, and expanded consciousness, we were *given* this gift of the Integrated Self Model through divine inspiration from God, Source, Spirit. In part 3, we share the story of how Patrick received inspiration spontaneously in 2009 about the Integrated Self Model and how he came across the information about fourteen years later at a time when mental health education was high, and many people reported and shared their spiritual awakenings more than ever. In this book, we offer you a roadmap to help you move forward in your efforts to connect with the next best version of yourself by finding balance and peace along your path through the human-spirit experience.

Overall, the single most significant and impactful concept that you will discover in this book as you start your journey is the concept of self-awareness. From awareness of Self, consciousness will emerge and expand. Through the pillars of choice and change, balance will appear and the benefits will be realized. When you experience the benefits of changing your energy, your mindset, and your behaviors to ones that feel more in alignment with your ego and soul, it gives you further assurance and determination to integrate these new pieces. Eventually, and maybe even for the first time, peace will be seen as a possibility and become visible on the horizon. The path to inner peace will come into view, into focus, as you follow the roadmap presented to you by this book (if you choose).

We always hear people say, "Life is about the journey, not the destination." People who have already reached their destination say that, or people who have at least reached a period of relief from the trials and tribulations where they can see things from the perspective of the moment, having made it through a difficult stretch of the journey. When you are in the throes of the journey, this can be extremely difficult to hear from someone, and it can also be very disheartening.

In reality,

> there is nothing easy about becoming conscious... Abdicating responsibility to an outside source can seem, at least for the moment, so much easier. Once you know better, however, you can't get away with kidding yourself for long... The journey toward becoming conscious is often more attractive in theory than it is in practice. Pursuing consciousness theoretically through books and conversations allows us to fantasize about getting to the promised land without actually having to make any changes in our lives. Even the thought that a promised land exists can temporarily make a person feel great.[6]

When life is good, we would like to believe that we have reached our ultimate destination of peace for which we have been searching, wanting, and needing. These little moments of peace serve as a brief pause in the journey that will allow us to take a much-needed breath before we continue on the journey of life. Thankfully for the two of us, we have reached points in our respective lives where inner peace is the prevailing energy and emotion during our days now that we have worked through a lot of our hardships, adversity, and even traumas that had us living in our own subconscious periods of anxiety, disappointment, and eventually hitting bottom realizing that there was no other way to go but up.

Now that we have been able to heal through our past, we actually believe the pain, lessons, and growth were essential to experiencing and appreciating the peace that we live in today. Living in peace allows you to breathe, expand, be who we truly are, and immerse energy into our purposes. By no means are we saying that we are free from experiencing obstacles, curveballs, and pain but being able to consciously evolve allows you to understand your Self and flow through these times with more ease, grace, and self-compassion,

> Transformation is a slow process, so don't be discouraged. Take as long as you need. Do be gentle with yourself and allow your heart, mind, and spirit to process the stories and lessons you've read before you return for more. Don't worry—your Authentic Self will guide you. And your search will be all the more fulfilling.[7]

Through this book, we share with you the topics of awareness, consciousness, and choice. The magnitude of these topics will largely depend on your current story, identity, thirst for truth, and hunger for growth. Wherever you are on the path of your life journey, we pass on to you this Model for balanced growth and conscious integration of your authentic Self.

You have the permission to give yourself a break and some grace. This may require you to have faith that you are not alone in this world, or in the universe. This may require you to believe that you are loved and that you are love, itself. This may require you to believe in miracles, that you are worthy of miracles, and that you are a miracle and magic for yourself and others. As you turn the page and embark on this journey with us, be ready to uncover and discover parts of your Self that have been long buried and hidden away. Be ready to connect with your consciousness, to your authentic Self, and to your Creator (whether you refer to as God, Source, Spirit, Allah, and so on). Be ready to experience the miracles of the human-spirit journey! So I ask you, are you along for the ride?

PART 2

Lessons of the Past and Keys to the Future (by Arianna)

Section 2.1—A New Perspective on Growth and Evolution

One thing that I believe we all have in common is that no matter your race, gender, education, social class, or spiritual beliefs, we all are trying to navigate this life and we all have faced adversity of some kind. I truly believe that we are all one, that no person is better than another, and that the work you do on yourself impacts not only yourself but also your family, your community, and the world. This book is intended to share a holistic perspective on growing and evolving through the hardships, traumas, and adversity that we are challenged by here in the world as spiritual beings having a human experience. Our intended focus is on the dualistic nature of our energy through balancing our divinity with our humanity, finding peace in both the light and dark, the soul and the ego.

Over the past couple of years, conversations of healing, mental health, consciousness, and spirituality have come to the forefront of social media as the world has changed drastically. During this time, many people have had what is commonly referred to as a spiritual awakening as truth is coming to light in our societies. As someone who has experienced a spiritual awakening many times myself, in addition to healing many of my childhood wounds, subconscious programming, and traumas, I felt certain that I was being called to support and guide those who are on this journey of growing and evolving from the past to live a life in authenticity, personal power, self-love, and inner peace.

Patrick and I have our own unique experiences and perspectives on healing with faith and have created a fluid model for those on this journey of self-development and soul evolution (that we will talk about in detail later in this book). In this part, I will share how I was able to integrate a new way of being (on an energetic level) to find peace in the light and dark aspects of myself by developing a conscious relationship with myself and God and becoming greater than my mind, body, and environment.

I feel compelled to point out that this work is not for everyone, and I do not mean that egotistically. Patrick and I very much acknowledge that there are many therapeutic approaches and holistic ways to heal and that this model and framework may not be for everyone. Much of this work includes developing skills such as introspection, discernment, and awareness which not everyone learns in the same way, nor may understand how to practice by watching Instagram reels. We highly encourage you to find some support along your path whether it is a therapist, coach, practitioner, or a community of like-minded people. We are of course not suggesting that "this is the only way," but instead we are providing a framework for personal growth for those who are inspired and have been looking for guidance for a place to start and self-evaluate.

Later in this book, you will read Patrick's history and tips for rewriting your story of the past, and in this section, you will be encouraged to dive into my personal world so you will come to know what challenges I faced, what I learned from them, and how I was able to heal into a genuine, authentic, confident woman from a past that did not support this version of her. We will then switch gears as we pivot into talking about the model we have created for you to use to guide yourself along your journey. I appreciate you for holding space for me here and I cannot wait to see what you take away from my journey and apply it to your own real-world experience in a uniquely, personalized way.

It's about time (in my opinion) that we stop separating faith from healing physically, emotionally, mentally, and energetically. I have seen countless people including myself have a massive shift when taking more of a holistic perspective on health. It has been frowned upon by many to mix science and spirituality; however, the overwhelmingly positive results speak for themselves. Science is ever-changing, and with the expanding research with alternative therapies, advancements in the fields of epigenetics and neuropsychology, as well as the increase in popularity in ancient practices of Ayurveda and Traditional Chinese Medicine, there is clearly more interest in other nontraditional perspectives of positive health.

Dr. Joe Dispenza states that if something happens once it is considered an incident, if the same thing happens two or three times it's a coincidence, and five or more times, it is considered a pattern.[8] There are thousands of people healing from their past conditioning and hardships through spirituality and holistic modalities today with incredible, genuine results. That shows that there is something needing to be explored here and a new discussion regarding science and spirituality is long overdue. I have studied topics such as quantum physics, neuroscience, subconscious reprogramming, Traditional Chinese Medicine, and emotional regulation, just to name a few. I am also continuing my education in this light to receive my Doctorate and PhD in Natural Medicine.

With an open mind and an open heart, I would like to now share with you how I overcame situations and environments that have shaped me into becoming someone I am not, and then how I was later led down a different path toward wholeness in mind, body, and spirit. I will first share some experiences, followed by the wisdom I had extracted, and then we will learn some key elements that I used to create balance and continue to evolve in mind, body, and spirit.

Section 2.2—Relatable Experiences and Keys of Wisdom

While I do not want to bore you with a comprehensive timeline of events, the way I would describe my childhood and young adulthood was influential. I will touch on some of the denser experiences from my past with the intention to perhaps provide new perspectives for those who relate, but please note that it wasn't all terrible. I have fond memories of my childhood and young adulthood that are sprinkled in between what I am about to share with you. I am grateful for always having food on the table, any pets we wanted, parents who would wake up at the darkest hour of dawn to drive me to my sports events, many vacations, and laughs. Healing isn't just for those that have had it really rough; healing is for everyone no matter how light or heavy your past was. Even though I remember being happy and free at some points, I also lived through restriction, suppression, and fear.

I had deeply impactful experiences of betrayal, manipulation, bullying, rejection, and abuse that I will forever remember. From a now unattached perspective, I am grateful for all these influences as I have learned so many lessons through living through these experiences, which have led me to transmute this pain into personal power and wisdom. All of these challenging situations have allowed me to see my strength and courage. I truly know that each experience that we have teaches us a lesson and provides us with an opportunity to grow moving forward. Let's dive into some of the things that I experienced and the key pieces of wisdom that I extracted, in no particular order or significance.

Bullying: I grew up with two brothers on a farm in Connecticut before moving to New York in the 4th grade. We were ecstatic about moving from a family farm to a neighborhood where we had friends all around us constantly. While I had the side of me that took dance classes and played with dolls and makeup, I also loved to play football and airsoft with the boys. I quickly started to notice in my new school that I did not fit in with the cool girls, wear the same clothes, or know any of the shows or music that I felt at the time were beyond our years (I guess I was a bit naive). Looking back, I naturally gravitated toward my natural interests, had my own small group of friends in the beginning, and enjoyed those times the most (the times when I trusted everyone around me and explored my natural passions).

I realized that I only started comparing myself to the other girls my age when they started making it known that I was not wanted or accepted or that it was not safe for me to be my natural self. I was bullied for the boy I expressed interest in, the instrument I played, and called out for dancing *weirdly* at our school dance. I had even experienced adults shaming me as a young teen for not expressing interest in their son (literally confronted by a mother who tried to get me to date her son) and guilting me for how much cream cheese was on my bagel. I have so many memories where behind closed doors I would be so passionate about what I was interested in doing, but once I shared my interest with classmates at school or they found out about it, it was thrown back in my face. This made me feel extremely uncomfortable and I started trying to conform to the norm in order to dissolve some of the comments, looks, and gestures. I would obsess about and overthink everything, even down to the binder I bought for school, and whether or not to accept a solo in band rehearsal (because that would have made me an easy target for gossip and criticism that I didn't need).

I began to notice that it was extremely difficult for me to trust other girls and I developed a love-hate relationship with them. I naturally (and protectively) assumed that every girl who had a high social standing or a loud personality was going to hurt me, but I desperately wanted the social validation they held. This made me feel like I had to do my best to befriend them. Over time, I became deeply insecure and separated from that young girl who did what she wanted naturally and didn't put herself in a box. I listened to the feedback I received from these girls and forced myself to play small, ultimately placing myself in a box that I was never meant to belong in. Although I would say my heart never went hard, the mask I wore to be more accepted also came with walls and triggers that kept me in a state of survival, all the while lacking boundaries and the education on how to navigate this new terrain or regulate myself. I developed mild social anxiety along with extreme insecurity, all buried beneath this mask of a responsible bookworm who has a couple of friends, keeps to herself, and doesn't dare speak her mind.

My experience of being bullied taught me that my authentic self is not accepted by those that had social power and that those same people can create a living hell for you if you say or do something they don't like. I learned that if I wanted to be left alone, I had to water down who I was, not attract attention to myself, and not "try" so hard. I developed guilt around my natural abilities and strengths such as loving school, getting good grades, taking my musical instrument seriously, and being my weird goofy self. I learned to alter who I was in certain environments and got very used to being this dimmed, watered-down, diluted version of myself.

Bullying was significant for me because it influenced the way I viewed myself. I lost connection to my authentic self, who was goofy, funny, smart, and multi-talented, all to become this serious, hyper-independent student afraid to show her true self. I knew that in order to survive, I had to become this *safe* version of myself, but it was so ingenuine that the lines were blurred between who I truly was and who I was becoming. Insecurity and anxiety became my new normal as I had to keep up the pretense of this personality that I knew subconsciously wasn't who I truly was. I became filled with resentment and sat in the truth (of my belief) that nobody liked me.

As I began developing self-awareness years later and started to hold space for myself and my feelings in my last two years of college, I realized that the more I was myself, the more I attracted true friends that felt like family. I started getting *glimmers* of what life could be like being accepted for my authentic self as I started making genuine connections. I got a taste of cracking a joke in front of a group, playing a game at a party with people watching, and giving presentations from a place of believing in myself. Encouraged by these positive social experiences, I began exploring my actual interests and what felt good to me such as becoming a campus EMT and doing genetic research with my biology professor.

The success, support, and love that I desperately needed were reflected back to me when I embraced being who I am, and I realized that for years I didn't show these parts of myself due to the bullying I had received in grade school. I began to understand that those who bullied me were projecting their own insecurities and fears onto me, whether it was intentional or unconscious to them because they noticed that I did not fit the common trends or molds or initially had the desire to be like them. Through a new perspective, I realized that their bullying tactics impacted me only because I took their comments and opinions as fact, and in turn integrated those beliefs into my identity.

This was just one of the examples in my life of learning that those who are jealous of us try to dim our light as a way to control us and thereby their own emotions by keeping us small, in a box, or with a label. I truly believe that we are so complex that labels cannot define our whole being, and placing someone in a box or with a label is a way for our human minds to provide a feeling of belonging. This ultimately limits all of us because we then only see the label, dismiss the aspects that do not align with that label, and forget that we can create our own label, or belong to a plethora of labels.

This whole time, I was trying to be like everyone else to avoid getting bullied and holding their opinions about me as true. I accepted their projections as fact in my mind which is why I believed them when they said I was weird or called me an overachiever. It wasn't until I started asking myself if these have been true, all to which I came to the answer (in a place of stillness) that I didn't actually believe these self-formed beliefs about myself. I realized from that place of stillness that these self-formed beliefs were in fact projections and expectations that I absorbed in a state of survival.

I began healing my self-concept (more on this later) and reprogrammed my mind and body to release these limiting beliefs that told me that who I am isn't enough, isn't desired, or accepted. I have shifted my energy to a frequency of confidence and self-worth, and I love myself like never before. I thank all past child versions of myself for enduring these harsh lessons in order for my adult self to heal and learn from them. Through this healing, I have connected to and come home to my authentic self with my own beliefs, thoughts, and behaviors that are true to me. I have accepted that I am different for a reason and that our differences are what make this world beautiful. I stopped striving to be perfect as I connected to my faith from a different perspective, realizing that everything from God has *imperfections*; God never makes mistakes.

The goal never was to be perfect; the goal is to be authentic, and who God made you to be. I realized that judging ourselves and others is directly judging God's work and beauty, so I've been on a mission to hold kindness, respect, and love for everybody no matter who you are. *Perfect* never existed, and those of us striving for it are looking for a destination that does not exist, nor is the point of this existence. I honor the light and dark within and rest in being the best version of myself no matter how that is perceived. I am open-minded to having conversations, exploring new perspectives, and admitting when I'm wrong (which is something I resisted for the longest time). When you begin to stop trying to be *perfect* and *right*, you open yourself up to new possibilities, conversations, wisdom, love, and self-acceptance.

Hypervigilance and people-pleasing: Unfortunately, a lot of adults place inappropriate expectations on children. With the expanded awareness that I now have, sometimes I cannot help but sigh when I see parents who cannot regulate their own selves, expecting their children to be able to. I have compassion for these individuals as I lived this myself, which is why it has been a personal goal of mine to address anything and everything from my past so that I do not pass it down or project it onto my future children. I do not expect to be a perfect parent, but instead, choose to educate myself and practice healthy ways to communicate and regulate my emotions so my children do not have to experience what I did.

Children learn by example and by demonstration. Children are the ultimate mirrors who reflect back to you what you are feeling. If you are an unregulated adult, how can you expect your child to handle their emotions when you are constantly modeling what dysregulation looks like? Children learn how to react emotionally to problems by watching how you handle problems and respond to stressors. When children feel emotions, we need to hold space for them and show them healthy ways to cope with and understand these feelings.

I grew up in a household where it was normal to get yelled at for spilling milk, making a mistake, or having the TV too loud. It was normal to be around people who were emotionally unpredictable and feared the consequences of any unfulfilled expectations. I had to grow up quicker in order to be able to evaluate my environment and course-correct problems before they became my problem. I lived in a constant state of "they're going to kill me if I don't do x, y, or z." Our parents were going through financial and marital struggles at times, and I felt constantly a victim to whatever their emotions happened to be. I was exposed to parental arguments with loud yelling, slamming doors, and the likely possibility of one parent leaving at the end of the argument without any idea where they were going and when they would come back. This left us with one parent in their post-argument emotional state, where we walked on eggshells constantly afraid to make a wrong move or ask a wrong question.

Not speaking for my siblings, I personally developed extreme people-pleasing tendencies as a way to be able to control my environment for my survival. I became a "second mother" to my younger brother who is seven years younger than me, taking on a role to defend and protect him at all costs (emotionally). I have a memory of holding him while we both cried as our parents were arguing, although I also have many memories of consoling him as his young brain tried to process what was going on around him.

There was a lot of exposure to marital problems that I shouldn't have known at such an early age. I felt responsible for maintaining my parent's emotions by doing extra around the house, getting super disciplined about my grades, and attacking any potential issues that I sensed could escalate into a huge problem before they were able to. I knew my parents were going through a lot and I'd like to say I never took sides; however, it was hard not to take sides knowing the intricate details of their arguments, and not being developed enough to process and make sense of it all.

I became hypervigilant and aware of my surroundings at all times, very attuned to people's energy and emotional states, "Hypervigilance is defined as the feeling of being constantly on guard for the purpose of detecting potential danger, even when the risk of danger is low."[9] My emotional triggers included yelling, loud noises, and getting overstimulated by technology if many sounds were being played simultaneously. I lived in survival mode, carrying many problems that weren't mine but knew I could alter the environment I was in by lessening any potential problem through my people-pleasing tendencies, "People-pleasing is the act of making others happy to avoid conflict or negative feelings—even if you don't like what you're doing."[10] Due to my low self-esteem and needing validation from external sources, I would try to be as responsible as I could around the house and in my personal endeavors, but I would also go out of my way to help others or do things without being requested in expectation of receiving a compliment or appreciation in some way.

Some say that people-pleasing is an act of manipulation because you are doing something in order to predict or alter a person's emotional state for your own personal benefit. What results is a relationship where you get used to creating an environment in order to receive validation or your desired response from that person, so your emotional void(s) are filled. When you feel that emotional void, you learn to manipulate the environment or do something to "please" someone so you receive your desired emotional fulfillment. People that are used to getting "pleased" by you, are under a false illusion that those actions are genuine. Most of the time, your subconscious or unconscious intention is that you have an unmet need that will be met by this person when you can create a situation to get it from them, not that you intentionally want to do these actions. People-pleasing is, in my opinion, a lack of personal autonomy where you get used to using other people or situations outside yourself to numb the feeling that you are avoiding within. When you stop pleasing them for your own benefit of emotional security, they sometimes perceive that as you not caring about them anymore, being rude, or inconsiderate as they are accustomed to receiving a certain treatment from you. At one point or another, people will start to see through the people-pleasing illusion of your actions.

Most of the time though, the acts of people-pleasing that we find ourselves doing are actually a sacrifice for our own well-being and not serving us in a real way. For example, I find so many times in my own life and with my clients that people feel obligated to accept an invitation to meet with someone or attend an event. Even though they don't want to go, they force themselves to because the thought of saying no to people is uncomfortable, and the fear of "letting people down" is at the forefront. The ego does not feel safe in knowing that people may have a "negative reaction" to your response of not going. So these people-pleasers go to events and parties knowing that they don't want to be there to show face and keep their reputation in good standing. I used to pride myself on being a people-pleaser before I truly looked at how this tendency came to be. I thought that it was admirable to constantly give without expecting anything in return until I realized that I was expecting validation in return. As someone who struggled with being accepted, I naturally would do anything anyone needed even if we weren't close in order to get that "Wow, thank you for picking me up!" or "It means so much to me that you're here!" validation of being seen and appreciated, which filled that hole of rejection and bullying from when I was a child. I desperately wanted to be seen as the super nice girl who would do anything for anyone at any time.

I fully understand this perspective that people-pleasing is manipulation, although it is important to note that people-pleasing tendencies are not normally created from a conscious place, therefore to me, not a conscious manipulation. Just like narcissism, people-pleasing is another coping mechanism to be able to control others around us after experiencing some type of trauma in order to maintain a sense of continuity, predictability, and safety. People-pleasing is a result of trying to keep yourself safe and accepted by making others feel good in some way. To say that it is manipulative may be correct, although it is more important to understand how and why you developed these tendencies and how you can begin to heal from them. Once you are aware that you have people-pleasing tendencies, it is your responsibility to acknowledge and accept that you had probably learned this behavior in order to protect yourself or receive validation in some way, and find ways to heal from these tendencies so you can live in autonomy and create genuine connections.

When I started becoming aware of my people-pleasing tendencies, I realized that I was unconsciously sacrificing so much of my time and energy for others, instead of using this energy to address the root cause of these tendencies. I realized that most of the time when I would be drawn to people-please, it was because there was a trigger or wound within me that, instead of choosing to observe and feel into the trigger or wound, I would fill the unmet need by performing an act of people-pleasing. Over time, this gets exhausting as you realize that you give so much of your energy away to things for a predictable outcome.

Through inner child healing, I became aware of my tendencies and no longer resonated with this way of behaving. Since this subconscious aspect was so hardwired in me from childhood, it was challenging to release and reprogram. I want to normalize that it can take months or even years to fully overcome such a subconscious behavior response, but it is 100 percent possible. As I became more confident in my authentic self and started pouring into my own cup (self-love), I no longer felt that I needed validation from others by going so far out of my way to receive it; the void within me was filled with self-love. I held space for my inner child as I began to realize that people-pleasing was a trauma response in order to be seen and safe, but I now have the ability to protect myself in healthy ways through creating boundaries with myself and others, reaffirming that I am always in control of myself and that I cannot control other people's emotions, perception, or response to what I do or how I live my life.

Rejection wounds: In addition to bullying, one of the reasons why I wasn't confident in myself as a young girl and eventually as a woman is because of the continuous rejection that I was very used to getting from men. From little crushes to middle school flings, I always would end up getting ghosted or "broken up with." I felt that I wasn't desirable enough to receive attention from men, so any time a boy expressed interest in me, I felt that I had to perform or maintain a certain persona to keep them interested. Most of the time, I never was given a reason as to why a boy all of a sudden lacked interest in me. I started to feel anxiety around men and lowered my standards.

I had one boyfriend in high school who went to a different school in my district but we made it work. I did feel accepted by him until he broke up with me out of the blue. Even though he came running back two weeks later, I was so heartbroken that I did not continue seeing him. I then almost immediately jumped into another relationship with another boy that truly felt like a fairytale in high school. After two years, it was time to pick colleges and I found it strange that he waited until the last minute to pick his college (later finding out that he was waiting to see where I would pick to ultimately follow me there). After two weeks of being in college together, he started acting strange and stopped eating. I knew something was wrong but he wouldn't allow me to call his parents. He eventually told me that he was sick with guilt because he had been cheating on me all summer and I suppose holding this secret was quite literally eating him alive.

Looking back at this time, I never cared about his confession because I was so worried about his mental and physical health. He moved back home and I sacrificed my first month of weekends at college by going home to check on him until I finally processed the truth of what happened and ultimately made the decision to break up with him. I stayed single and focused on my friend group for the rest of freshman year. During this time being single, I received a lot of attention from men which was the opposite of what I had experienced prior. I found myself drawn to men who were arrogant, untrustworthy, and demonstrated that they had almost no respect for women. I started exclusively seeing someone who eventually told me that he was not a relationship type of guy and that my feelings that I had for him were not reciprocated, leaving me once again heartbroken and rejected for what turned out to be the last time.

About two months later when I felt checked out from romantic relationships, I passed by the college's baseball team in the dining hall where they were eating lunch, and my eyes locked with one of the guys but I didn't know his name or anyone else on the team. While I kept wondering who he was, I wasn't in the mental space to chase anyone especially as we were entering finals week before summer vacation. My friends jokingly helped me get Tinder without any intention to meet this man, but rather more of a way for us to swipe together and hang out without any real expectations.

On Tinder, I saw the man I locked eyes with in the dining hall and swiped right, leading him to message me shortly after. We immediately started getting to know each other and realized that we came from the same high school district so we didn't have to travel long distances if we wanted to see each other over the summer while home from college. I am still with my college sweetheart today and believe with every bone in my body that God placed him in my path on purpose, and with purpose, to prevent a downward spiral or repeated cycles with men. I have learned so much from this man, and I continue to learn from him as he carries so much patience, Grace, and unconditional love within himself for me to witness and experience.

In all the fairytales and movies, women are shown that we're supposed to get this butterfly feeling and act all crazy around the love of our life. We're supposed to act differently and try harder to keep them hooked; that we know a man is right for us when we lose all sense of reality and can't breathe around them. I knew my boyfriend was different from any other man I've ever known when I met him in person because I didn't feel butterflies or anxiety, actually quite the opposite. My nervous system was calm, it was finally safe and at home. There was stillness like the water of a pond when it was so calm that it looked like glass. To this day, I find his energy incredibly grounding and safe. I don't have to be anything other than myself; he has never judged me, has been my biggest supporter, and gives me the space to be my weird, expressive self.

While I may never understand why I experienced so much rejection, I believe that rejection is redirection; God kept redirecting me until I crossed paths with the man God made for me. I am grateful for all the relationships and times my heart was broken because I learned so much about myself and what I do and don't want when it comes to romantic relationships. I learned all the red flags and behaviors that I did not want in my next partner as well as the areas that I could improve upon in maintaining a relationship with someone else. I look at it now as a time of preparation for when the man of my dreams crosses my path because they will, and he did. Since I experienced so much let-down, I finally was able to recognize a good man when I saw one; one who carried respect, genuine confidence, and humility but also was able to express vulnerability, crave adventure, and truly value me, the authentic me. Our relationship gets stronger as every year passes and we continue to work on our communication, boundaries, and active listening.

This relationship has taught me all the false ideals I held about dating and romantic relationships. I personally don't think that anyone is perfect, but with the right person you can learn to grow, let your walls down, express yourself and your needs, and create healthy boundaries. We are shown as a society that you're automatically supposed to just *click* with someone on every level and not have to work in the relationship. A relationship will never be consistently fifty-fifty; it's about finding the person who can recognize when you only have twenty to give, and will gracefully pick up the remaining eighty without contention. It's learning to flow through life together and building the skills within the relationship to have a solid foundation so that when life hits the fan, you work together and lean on each other. Find someone who you can share your secrets with, who when things are hard or amazing they're the first person you're running to, who your nervous system feels safe with, and someone who never dims your light.

Playing small: One of the things I noticed early on when I began to heal from some of these other wounds is that I came to realize how challenging it was for me to speak up, express myself, or explain myself to others. I realized that there had also been a pattern growing up seemingly familiar in family, school, and even with friends where I was constantly silenced, hushed, or quieted. I can also recall times when I would express my beliefs or feelings all to be disagreed with or left to feel like my perspective was wrong. While I learned to stay quiet and small from bullying, I have memories of going to adults for advice or to share my opinion where I was immediately pushed to the side, or guilted into changing my opinion. I remember trying to break up with a *boyfriend* in middle school and his mother pulled me aside to tell me how disrespectful that was and how much I was hurting her son. I have memories of more emotionally sensitive situations, such as funerals where I expressed feeling scared to walk up to the casket and being dismissed, and where I was scolded for covering my ears during the loud gunshots in a military funeral.

Over time, I learned that it was not worth the effort to speak my mind or stand up for myself after many experiences of no one taking me seriously or caring as much as I needed. I began questioning myself and I was unable to fully trust my own opinions and feelings. I soaked in any consequence and stopped expressing my true feelings as I learned that it wouldn't change my situation. The more I wasn't allowed to express my true feelings, the more I realized that I had to deal with them myself, and the more I realized that most adults couldn't express their feelings either. This led to carrying a lot of resentment and anger within me as I had no outlet to express myself, nor did I have an example of how to regulate and deal with my emotions.

I learned that I was constantly expected to be of service to the emotions of authority figures, but the second that I expressed any emotion myself, it was a problem that was reacted to by those same authority figures with dysregulated emotions. It became apparent to me that these authority figures expected something of me that they couldn't demonstrate themselves.

Through healing from this conditioned silence, I have come to understand that people do the best with what they know. People can only meet you as far as they have met themselves, and unfortunately, as a young girl, I experienced staying quiet, told to not make waves, and that there would be consequences if you speak your mind as no one wanted to deal with a girl with her own opinions. In doing some reflection I also realized that it is possible that the adults that quieted me were trying to avoid their own insecurities, such as getting strange looks or comments from other people. Putting myself in their shoes and considering their level of knowledge at the time, it makes complete sense why I was treated in certain ways, and I hold nothing but forgiveness and compassion for myself and others who influenced me this way.

The wisdom from these experiences is that I believe I was supposed to experience the contrast of what is now actually a superpower of mine. I allowed people to dim my light and quiet me out of fear of not being accepted or fear of the consequence of having something to say. I believe God wanted me to know what it felt like to have my voice suppressed and experience the response of others disagreeing with me so I could overcome that in order to be confident in speaking my truth and encourage others to do the same, as that is a large part of my purpose. God taught me that when people are trying to quiet you, speak louder. If people do not like what you have to say (as long as it is truly from love) then they're either not ready to hear what you have to say, or perhaps not the right audience, but that shouldn't stop you from speaking up. God taught me not to lower my opinion or intelligence to make others comfortable, and that you don't need to be liked, have the same opinion as everyone else, or have the same path. From all of this, I learned to express my truth, listen to my intuition, and regulate my emotions.

Religious programming: I was born into a Catholic family where we went to church and took church classes through grade school. Looking back at my early memories in the church, it wasn't a warm, welcoming place to me. I don't remember anyone ever being happy or excited to go to church so I began picking up on the obligatory nature of going. I always envisioned God as a loving, inclusive Being with a sense of humor, who wanted the best for us and wanted to connect with each and every one of us individually. I believed that the world was magical and that with God's help, miracles existed. But when I stepped foot in the church, I couldn't help but feel judged by the constant reminders that we are sinners and began to feel like I had to be a perfect human being in order for God to love me or see me.

When we moved to New York, I continued my Catholic classes toward receiving my Confirmation. I remember having slight arguments with my parents about how I didn't resonate anymore with these classes and begged them to let me stop going. I felt that through the church, I was taught that God's love was conditional, that it was a sin to want a great life, and that if you didn't follow their rules, you would spend an eternity in hell. That, along with the church's teachings that sex before marriage, and same-sex couples were sins, I began to feel even more separated from God as my inner knowing of what I believed God to be was not being demonstrated or encouraged in the church.

My father did sympathize with me but encouraged me to finish the last year of classes in case I ever wanted to get married in a church or return to this religion at any time; I would at least be confirmed. Although I wasn't happy with this suggestion at the time, I do appreciate him looking out for me and considering my future decisions (although I now believe that you don't need anything besides a genuine relationship with God if you'd like to get married under his blessing). I was confirmed by the church as a senior in high school and went off to college where I never really thought about God, didn't pray, nor did I seek any alternative ways to work on my relationship with God.

At this time, I would say I was "separated" from God, although I don't believe we ever are. I just knew that I didn't resonate with what I've known all my life and had no idea what else was out there for me regarding practicing and connecting to my faith. I was also a premed major at the time and had barely any time to even immerse myself in a hobby or put my attention toward this. I did notice throughout this time that I was not close to God, I was extremely stressed and fearful, and a lot of my anxieties such as fearing death came to the surface. Reflecting back, this time in my life when I was least connected to God was the most unstable time of my life emotionally, physically, and mentally. I slowly started creating my own relationship with God as I neared the end of my undergraduate degree and built a practice of faith over time that has no label, no rules, and is based on unconditional love from the God I always believed in. Some could call me spiritual, although that is just another label that comes with judgments and certain ideals.

The concept of spirituality that I think is widely misunderstood is that spirituality is not a religion. People enter spirituality and try to treat it like a religion, but it is actually a free practice with many different existing kinds of beliefs and practices. Everyone is unique in their view of God, the Universe, and Source, at the same time. It encourages free thinking, and free connection to the Divine without a specific time and location like many religions do. This is because spirituality teaches that God is within every single one of us, as we are pieces of God. Therefore, God is never separate from you in spirituality but within you, and God is waiting for you to remember that and shine your light.

I've never felt more at home and accepted by such a community where you'll find so many different kinds of practices, methods, and beliefs, but everyone (for the most part) is accepting wherever you lie.

Coming from a religion that I found to be highly restrictive, I finally found my home and freedom by connecting to God through my own belief system that I created based on my connection to Source, Mother Gaia, my ancestors, and angels (supported by the signs and synchronicities that I would receive along my unique path). I'm one who is not quick to label or fit myself into a box (I've had enough of that). So for the sake of this book and for understanding, I would say I am spiritual, but instead of jumping into the spiritual community and taking everything as fact, I chose to witness many perspectives before coming home to my beliefs in which I have grounded myself.

I completely respect anybody's relationship with God whether you label it or not. My goal is to not have to prove that my belief system is correct or better than anyone else's belief system as everyone should be allowed to connect to the Divine in their own way. I believe that there is no such thing as *wrong* or *right* but instead different timelines, paths, and perspectives to explore with an open mind. The point I am trying to make is that many of us are indoctrinated to believe certain things from a young age that we don't ever stop to question, whether that is something that is expanding our lives or limiting us. When we don't actually believe in our belief system is when you come across those who *claim* they live a life in faith but their actions do not demonstrate that.

I understand we as human beings can get triggered in such a sensitive conversation, and our egos want to prove something. I want to normalize that you are free to change your mind and change directions whenever you want. You can change your beliefs whenever you want (you just have to be open to new perspectives). I know there are many people out there that may be confused about what they believe, or feel that maybe there's more than what they've always known. That is why we created the Integrated Self Model that can help you create and solidify your own belief system freely and evolve your soul while staying balanced and grounded in this human experience.

I believe that the ultimate goal is to be able to lay your head down at night knowing what you believe in wholeheartedly, thinking and acting from that belief system, and simultaneously being able to hold space for others and accept that not everyone resonates with your belief system. I will share more about the foundational aspects of my belief system in a later section.

Section 2.3—The First Step Toward Growth

Now that you have had a peek into some parts of my past along with the wisdom these experiences have provided me, let's now dive into the key pieces and concepts that were crucial for me to start addressing some of these wounds and take steps toward balanced growth. When I graduated from undergrad in 2020, I had a plan to become a registered nurse but I felt misaligned on this path for many reasons and ultimately decided not to pursue it. I wanted to help people in a more positive way without being confined to a building or working for someone else. At this time, I had my very first spiritual awakening and started seeing myself from a higher perspective, not as the insecure, reactive, quiet woman that I learned to be in survival mode. A spiritual awakening is when you have a shift in consciousness where you no longer perceive yourself solely through your ego and constructed identity, but recognize that you have a soul that is driven by other motives (more on this later).

Now that I was home from college with no plan for my future in addition to the chaotic state of the world, I had more time to observe and notice who I was acting, thinking, and behaving as, and I concluded that my current perceived identity was not aligned with the version that I envisioned myself becoming. I always saw my future self as a free, outgoing, confident, loving woman but I was still consumed with resentment, insecurity, and judgment about myself and others. With my perception of the world and my future completely turned upside down, in addition to the realization that I was not acting or feeling in accordance with who I wanted to be, I vowed to myself that I would work to become that version of myself that was authentic, genuine, and confident.

The first step if you are looking to grow in your relationship with yourself is realizing that you have an ego and a soul, and you will need to work on developing awareness of both. These are two aspects of the human Self that are seemingly in opposition to each other (especially at the beginning of this work) because your ego wants to keep you safe, is fear-driven, rooted in lack, and focused on doing things and being logical. Whereas the soul is intuitive, focused on abundance and possibility, and craves presence, and passion. My ego screamed when I withdrew from nursing school because I chose to walk away from what was familiar, what was stable, and what would be the more logical, safe path for me. However, I could not ignore my soul telling me that there was a better path out there for me, but this path was unstable, unknown, and unconventional. This is where I experienced the most polarity when it came to the balance between the ego and soul. My soul was pulling me one way, and my ego was trying to anchor me into familiarity, safety, and predictability.

In the Integrated Self Model, you will notice that we demonstrate the different steps that the ego and soul go through as you evolve each aspect. We will learn more about that later, but I would like to emphasize that these are not concrete steps. Your ego and soul can go as fast or as slowly through these steps and even fall back down to the bottom to begin again as you expand your consciousness and find that old foundations have to crumble in order for new ones to form (so these steps are fluid in nature). The beautiful thing about living this human experience is that both the ego and the soul provide value, and the more you become aware of each aspect, the more you can evolve both in balance to a point where the ego no longer opposes the soul, but both work together in unison and both are accepted, integrated, and acknowledged. There is a hot debate online where many think the ego is evil and the more you evolve, the more the ego dies and you live purely from your soul essence.

While I understand this perspective, I have a little bit of a different opinion; it is not actually that the ego dies permanently, but evolves to support the soul over time as it is always present. The ego can go through many "ego deaths" to restructure itself in its beliefs. However, I want to stress that the ego is part of our human mind and therefore cannot be discarded. I find that the more you toss the ego to the side, the more it actually speaks louder and creates imbalance because you are not allowing yourself to witness it.

Creating balance between the ego and soul does not mean you have to always follow the ego, but rather listen and acknowledge the concerns that it brings up. When I disenrolled from nursing school I sat there in the fear of the unknown that my ego was bringing to light, but also witnessed my soul telling me that this was the right path for me. I believe that there is no *right* or *wrong* decision, so I could have listened to my ego and taken the safe route and probably lived a stable life as a nurse. Instead, I chose to trust my soul as uncomfortable as it was to move into the fear of the unknown without a plan. I chose to continue along my path trusting that I would find something more fulfilling to me than nursing could provide. Looking back, I'm so grateful my past self followed in blind faith, as I have found my passion and fulfillment in this work.

My belief is that there is value in being a human being, and our humanistic traits are essential. While the ego may represent darkness, the dark is meant to be integrated, as you illuminate it with your light (meaning that you become aware of its existence and choose to accept it). To live completely from our soul and reject anything that makes us human is not the purpose of learning and growing through this experience.

As mentioned, the first step in growth is to develop self-awareness, "Self-awareness represents the capacity of becoming the object of one's own attention. In this state, one actively identifies, processes, and stores information about the self."[11] In order to develop self-awareness, the major key to understanding is that you are not your mind or your body; you are the consciousness that observes both. You are pure consciousness, pure energy that is capable of observing itself from a nonjudgmental point of view where you allow yourself to think and feel whatever is natural at that time, but you don't judge yourself for that.

By becoming the observer of ourselves from a higher perspective, we can identify the thoughts, feelings, and actions that are aligned with our authentic selves and those that are not. Self-awareness requires us to not side with either the ego or the soul, but instead neutrally observe both to make aligned decisions and actions. For example, by becoming the observer of my thoughts, feelings, and actions, I was able to recognize that in survival mode I was very used to being in control. Any time that life threw me a curveball or I couldn't control something that was happening, I would react with impatience, frustration, and theatrics.

When I allowed myself to observe this happening from a neutral place, I understood why this was my natural reaction programmed from the past, but was aware that this was not serving me. This act of self-awareness helped me identify something to work on to move toward improving my patience, responses, and sense of control. This is different from the victim mentality I was living, where if something didn't go my way, my reaction was from a disempowered state of "How could this happen to me?" and instead is now, "Why is this happening for me? What can I learn from this?"

Without self-awareness, we are allowing ourselves to just exist from whatever conditions and programming we have endured and haven't assessed up until that point. This means that you are not consciously living, not open to new thoughts, and behaving based on intrinsic automatic responses, experiencing the same results. By developing self-awareness and choosing to observe the way you think, act, and behave, you are using your consciousness to be an active participant in your life and actually create desired outcomes by aligning yourself to who you want to become, instead of reliving the same cycles from the program that is currently running subconsciously for you. To live a conscious life is a choice, and the more you practice self-awareness and reflection, the more you get to know yourself and pinpoint areas of improvement for you to live a life that feels authentic and natural to you.

Section 2.4—Everything Is Energy

Another perspective shift that helped me embrace change and growth is that everything is energy; your thoughts, feelings, money, material items, nature, and body are all energy and that energy can manifest into matter. There are infinite possibilities of outcomes that we can experience at all times, and the outcome that you experience is a result of your intention (thought) and feeling (emotion). Dr. Joe

Dispenza expands on this topic further to say that humans are electromagnetic beings, meaning that we hold an electromagnetic signature that broadcasts to the universe, the quantum field, God, the Divine (whatever you believe in) our belief of what is possible, what we expect to happen. This "field" or universe, reflects back to us the electromagnetic signature that we broadcast, and we receive back what we put out through our intentions and feelings.

The next imperative question is, What comprises this electromagnetic signature? Think of your thoughts as electrical pings that carry conscious intention, and your feelings magnetize that experience or reality back to yourself. For example, if I am applying for jobs and I am thinking a thought such as "No one is going to want to hire me, I'm not that special," I am also probably feeling the corresponding feeling of insecurity around my ability to perform and possibly feeling inadequate. The electromagnetic signature and the energy that I am sending to the universe in this situation is that I have little to no faith that I will receive a job offer, and therefore closed off and not immersing my energy into any other outcome, so I may experience that expression of lack being reflected in my reality by not receiving a job offer because the universe mirrors back to us what we believe to be true.

Newtonian physics teaches us that reality is predictable and that we have to wait for something outside of us to produce a change inside of us. For example, you wait for the wealth to show up to then be grateful for it; that seeing is believing. This old way of viewing science through Newtonian physics is outdated in my opinion as it lies in the paradigm that we are all victims to whatever happens to us, and that we as humans have no effect on our external reality. Quantum physics brings about a new paradigm where the subjective mind has an effect on the objective world; that believing is seeing. You can actually change how you think and feel by altering the operating system (the subconscious) to believe that your desired experience has already happened, therefore magnetizing (or commonly known as manifesting) your desired reality and outcomes. Essentially, there are unlimited outcomes that can happen for you in every moment, and imagine yourself picking your desired outcome from all the possibilities, and then embodying the identity of the person who already is living that desired outcome.

Going back to the previous example of applying for jobs, there are infinite possibilities that can occur if you observe them and put your energy into that desired outcome. Now that we know the subjective mind can influence an objective world, we can choose the outcome that we will get the job within a week. During this time, you can alter your state of being to program the mind and body to believe that it has already received the job offer. Your conscious intention can be something like "Wow how did I get so lucky with my new job so quickly!" along with embodying the feelings that that version of you that receives the job offer would feel; maybe relieved, excited, accomplished. Now your electromagnetic signature (the belief) that you are putting out into the universe is that you have already accepted the job, magnetizing that possibility to yourself and into your reality by living as if it has already happened.

When I was becoming aware of the thoughts, feelings, and actions that were programmed from the past, I also began envisioning what my future self looked like. I made a list of differences between who I was living as now, and who I wanted to become in detail. Knowing that everything is energy and that there are more possibilities available to us if we open our minds to them, I knew it was now time to explore this programmed way of being and address all the shadows that were holding me back from embodying this new version of myself unapologetically.

Let's now explore how you can genuinely embody this new state of being by reprogramming your operating system (the subconscious) and learning to accept our shadows. A lot of coaches and practitioners in this field solely focus on just faking it until you make it, by just choosing to embrace a new identity; however, I fully believe that if you do not look at your shadow aspects and accept the past experiences, you will never genuinely feel how you want to or live the reality you are desiring because our shadows will always be there in the subconscious triggering old thoughts and feelings until we shine our light upon them.

Section 2.5—The Operating System, Self Concept, and Shadow Work

In the crucial time from birth to about the age of seven years old, our subconscious mind is like a sponge. We learn from our caregivers and form beliefs about the world, society, and ourselves based on what is modeled to us. These beliefs are further strengthened and *hardwired* into the subconscious as we grow older and see our reality reflect these beliefs back to us. Our subconscious may learn that "money is the root of all evil," "the harder you work the more successful you will be," or even learn that we have to be cautious of what we eat to maintain a figure, or that life is naturally hard and everything is expensive.

These conditions that we learn from our environment slowly become our beliefs as we learn to navigate the world around us and may even find external confirmation that these beliefs are true. From these beliefs, we see people and situations through this perspective lens, assigning positive or negative meaning to things. The disconnect comes when we are presented with a situation where our beliefs are challenged such as experiencing someone who is rich and a good person when you believe that all rich people are evil, or when we find that our beliefs are in the way of (and no longer align with) what we want to do, where we want to go, or how we want to feel.

Our beliefs are held in the subconscious mind that we operate from at least 90 percent of the time, as the subconscious is the automatic program from childhood if not addressed or changed. The subconscious includes the mind and the body, as the body is the unconscious mind. This is why people say, "Your mind may not remember, but your body does." Your nervous system (the body) learns from your experiences to keep you safe. From these beliefs that we have absorbed, we think thoughts that invoke an emotion, and then act or make a choice from that emotion. For example, I learned from a young age that my authentic self is not accepted, slowly began to believe this was true, and from this belief, I had corresponding thoughts of "I can't say that because nobody will agree with me," invoking an emotion such as insecurity and then making the choice not to share my opinion.

Our beliefs are what create our reality because from our beliefs, we feel and act in accordance, which brings a specific experience and outcome. If you find that your beliefs are not supporting you, and you wish to experience something differently, we must change the beliefs at the subconscious level in order for the operating system of the subconscious to learn to integrate a new way of being. Dr. Joe Dispenza states that two things happen when you cross the river of change from one set of beliefs to another; unlearning and relearning.[12] You must unlearn the beliefs, thoughts, feelings, and behaviors from the old self-identity, and relearn a new way of thinking, feeling, and behaving. We have to become conscious of the subconscious beliefs, thoughts, and behaviors that are not aligned with our authentic selves and learn to operate in a new way by showing the mind and body new beliefs, thoughts, and feelings.

Neurons in the brain that fire together, wire together, meaning that the more you can install a new way of operating, the more the brain will strengthen these neural connections. Neural patterns that are not being used naturally break down over time as the brain realizes that you no longer need that neural pattern. The concepts of unlearning and relearning are essentially consciously choosing not to think those old thoughts of "I am not good enough" or "I'll never be successful" so the brain starts to break them down, and choose to think and strengthen new neural connections by thinking new thoughts of "I am worthy of everything I desire" or "Success is possible for me, just like it is for everybody else."

Self Concept and Shadow Work in my opinion go hand in hand when it comes to growing from your past experiences and choosing a new way of being. Your self-concept is the way you view yourself and who you see yourself as. My subconscious learned from my past experiences that I had to alter my natural state of being to be liked and accepted, that I had to serve others around me in order to be appreciated, and that I had to keep my thoughts and opinions to myself. My self-concept (the way I viewed myself) was unlikeable, too weird, and insecure.

In order to change the way you view yourself, you have to address your shadows through shadow work. Through shadow work, you learn to face and accept all those parts of yourself that you reject, don't like, or don't want anyone to see. Shadow work takes honesty in being able to sit with yourself and in those uncomfortable feelings and experiences that you have possibly tried to suppress and call them all back to yourself, taking ownership of this energy and past versions of yourself.

Through shadow work, I accepted everything about myself that made me feel embarrassed, ashamed, undesirable, or undeserving. I learned that the aspects of myself that I was so used to rejecting like my innocence, goofiness, and my unique opinions were actually aspects of myself that grew on me the more I assigned my own meaning and value to them. I began to realize that the reason why I casted these aspects of myself away was because others had conditioned me to believe that they were bad and unwanted.

By defining my own worth and forming an idea of what my authentic self is, and what subconscious thoughts and fears are holding me back, I started reparenting my subconscious anytime these self-doubts or fears came up, and reminded myself of the new beliefs I wanted to embody. The unlearning and relearning typically happen at the same time, where you acknowledge where the past self is still present, and how you can start embodying the new self. I used holistic practices such as affirmations, meditation, and breathwork to reparent my nervous system as it would react with fear or anxiety at times when I would challenge myself to put myself out there or to think a confident thought.

The most important thing to remember is that you are unlearning and relearning at the same time, so it is important to be honest with yourself, not rush the process, and be kind to yourself. Do not run from fear but face it head on. Do not ignore or suppress it because it will come back around. You are teaching your subconscious a new way of being that is so strongly in place from years of confirmation. It is normal to jump back and forth between the old self and the new self as you find your footing and learn to have different thoughts, feelings, and choices.

I highly recommend when you do this work in the beginning, do it in a safe place so your mind and body get a taste of these new thoughts and feelings before you go out in the real world. It is important for your mind and body to be exposed to new thoughts and feelings and spend time in a new electromagnetic signature. For myself, I would play some meditation sounds while doing breathwork and would think the thoughts that I wanted my new self to think, and feel into feelings such as confidence, safety, and self-love. I would reaffirm to myself that I am safe and I am loved to experience feelings of self-empowerment and personal autonomy over my environment and body.

One step that you can take in growing your self-concept is observing your self-talk. Self-talk is the way we talk to ourselves in our head and you'd be surprised at some of the nasty things that you are telling yourself daily that are further confirming your subconscious beliefs. Become aware of when you say negative things to yourself or out loud like "I'm so stupid," "I'm broke," "I can't do that." When you pay attention to your self-talk, you can become aware of what those underlying thoughts and feelings are. Choose a new way of thinking, and remember that your words and thoughts hold power and energy that broadcast to the universe what you think and believe. I would giggle to myself when I first started reflecting on self-talk where I would affirm on the golf course, "I'm going to suck," and then inevitably I did. Start to become your own best friend, your ride-or-die, your own biggest cheerleader. Celebrate your small wins when you identify a feeling or a thought, when you challenge yourself to grow, and when you use your light to illuminate a shadow.

We live in a world of dark and light, but we do not have to be afraid of the dark. You are the one that assigns a positive or negative meaning to something. Darkness does not exist in the light, and the more that we fear the darkness, the more that we run from it and create an imbalance internally. The shadow is the greatest teacher to expand your light as one makes the darkness conscious. Wholeness is experienced when one accepts the light and dark aspects of self and embraces it all. We are both light and dark, and just as you need the light to cast a shadow, you need darkness to appreciate the light.

Section 2.6—Emotional Intelligence

Emotional intelligence is an important skill to learn and develop if you want to have a healthy relationship with yourself and others. One of the most impactful reasons why a lot of people are so miserable, stressed, and not in love with themselves and their lives is because we ignore our feelings, but forget that they will keep coming back around until you address them. I used to be this type, where anytime I had an intense emotion, I felt uncomfortable and would suppress it by pretending I didn't feel that way, would numb it with alcohol, or project from that emotion, which in turn affected my relationships.

As stated before, emotions are energy in motion. By looking at our emotions in a new way of energy moving through us as a result of something in our external environment or something like a thought from within our internal environment, we can start to identify triggers to our emotions and also identify the emotions that we feel. If you are someone who struggles with understanding your emotions, the first step is to allow yourself to actually feel them. There is a lot of debate online about emotional regulation, and people believe they have to intellectualize their emotions. Your number one job when you feel anything is to sit with that feeling and then try to identify it. When we can feel our emotions as they come up, we are allowing and accepting that energy to move through us instead of pushing our feelings down to be dealt with later (yes, they will keep coming up until you face them). Knowing that this feeling is just an energy moving through you, you do not have to attach yourself to it; just allow yourself to feel it without judgment.

For example, let's say that my friend and I apply separately to win an all-inclusive vacation. My friend ends up calling me to say that she won and that she is going to bring her husband with her. Immediately, I start to have an emotional reaction to this news, feel my energy shift, sort of congratulate her, and abruptly hang up the phone. I sit in that feeling that's super uncomfortable and allow it to be there, and spend time with it. After a while, you may be able to identify that it is jealousy that you are feeling. When we attach our thoughts to our emotions it may be something like, "Ugh, it's so gross that I am jealous. She is my best friend and I'm supposed to be happy for her. Why am I like this?" That is you attaching yourself to your jealousy and assigning it a negative meaning, bringing along other emotions like shame and guilt. Instead, when we identify that it is the emotion of jealousy, we can think a kinder thought that allows us to accept and hold space for ourselves such as, "Oh, I guess I feel some jealousy that she won, and I didn't."

Now we can stay in this energy of self-acceptance by continuing to be honest with ourselves. This may look something like, "I am a human being that is supposed to feel my emotions. I understand what I am feeling and I hold space for myself now as I feel jealous. This is something that I would like to work on moving forward as I know my future self is someone who gives her friends her flowers and is genuinely happy for others' wins as well as her own. Blessings are all around me, and maybe I can start to actively find ways and tap into the possibility of my husband and I going on a vacation together, as I find that that is what I desire." This is a large difference from the prior reaction, as now you are empowering yourself, solution-focused, not attaching yourself to jealousy, but instead open to what it is teaching you. Chances are if you choose this latter perspective, you will not feel guilt or shame for being jealous, as you have allowed yourself to explore what you desire from this situation.

Since emotions are energy in motion, you may notice that emotions such as guilt, shame, despair, fear, and jealousy are widely considered low vibrational energy, while feelings of peace, acceptance, confidence, and love are high vibrational. I'd like to do a little exercise with you now for you to notice the difference in energy. Pick a situation or outcome that you may be guilty of and take some time to feel that. For example, I may feel into the experience of cheating on a math test when I was in grade school. The energy of guilt feels contractive, restrictive, and limiting; maybe you feel heavy, dense, or that you cannot breathe well. Now shift your attention onto an experience of love, like snuggling your pet or your child. The energy of love is expansive and limitless; you may feel lighter like you're floating or that you can expand your chest and breathe deeply.

Toxic positivity is essentially the concept where people advise you to be in those higher vibrational emotions because they are expansive and limitless. However, there is so much to learn from feeling the contrast in the lower vibrational emotions. The higher emotions would not feel as activating if we hadn't experienced the lower ones. Human beings feel emotion, and no matter how evolved you are or what you are going through, we flow through different emotions daily. If you happen to fall into a lower vibrational emotion allow yourself to observe, address, and feel it. After a lot of healing, most of the time, I find myself peaceful, content, in flow, in alignment, but again, that does not mean that nothing ever stresses me out, nothing gets under my skin, and nothing ever bothers me. (Would I even be human if that's the case?)

You have the choice to feel whatever you want to feel. You could choose right now at this moment to feel peaceful, to feel love, to feel abundant, or you can choose to feel sad, upset, or frustrated. Instead of now walking around as a victim to your environment and to what is going on around you, you get to choose the perspective and the corresponding emotion you desire because you now understand (I hope) that you are always in control of your thoughts and feelings. Everything that you want to feel can be felt right now.

We as humans are indoctrinated into believing that we'll be happy once we have the money, the house, the children, and the perfect career; that external and material things provide us the feelings we want to feel once we have them. You could have not a dime to your name, no family, and no house but could choose to feel abundant. Material things can make us feel certain emotions, of course, but you do not need them to make you feel happy, fulfilled, or safe. Everything that you want to experience in your external reality must be observed and experienced in the internal first. If you want to have financial freedom what does that feel like? Feel that. If you want to have time freedom, what does that look like and feel like? Spend time with that energy.

As you grow and expand your consciousness, you will naturally raise your vibrational frequency (as your true frequency is naturally high), and you will be able to tolerate more, adapt quicker, and feel less stress. Emotional intelligence provides us the tools to hold space for ourselves to feel our feelings, not judge ourselves for what we feel, and learn how to eventually transmute that energy into an energy that is desired, commonly known as alchemy (all of course after addressing any growth that may be trying to present itself to you through these emotions).

The more you can learn to sit with your feelings, the less they get stuck in the body and become a part of your subconscious programming influencing your thoughts and behaviors. I know it can be difficult at first to sit in the grief, the pain, the guilt, or the shame, but it is also courageous and admirable to take accountability and face them instead of fearing them, which can create imbalance, stress, irrational behaviors, and projection onto others.

My beautiful stepmother has taught me a lot, and one thing I always hear her saying in my head is "Hurt people hurt people," and "healed people heal people." When we are not taking accountability for our emotional state, we tend to react from that emotion, hence, "hurt people, hurt people." When we are able to recognize that we are in a heightened emotional state and choose not to project from that emotion, hold space for ourselves, and communicate from a place of honesty and emotional maturity, we can create a healthy environment for ourselves and our loved ones, and embody the expression, "healed people, heal people."

Section 2.7—The Foundation of Your Belief System

The last discussion that I would like to share with you before we pivot to the Model, is how I unlearned and relearned a new belief system rooted in possibility, unconditional love, and direct communication with God and the Divine. The first thing that I started to do was see God in everything and everywhere. I knew that God is an omnipresent being that is everywhere and nowhere at the same time, meaning that I could connect with God whenever and wherever I wanted. I slowed down and tried to keep my attention on the present moment as much as possible so that I wasn't living in the past or worrying about the future, and began seeing God all around me. I saw

God in the grass, the birds, the flowers, the sun's energy, the wind, my pets, and my boyfriend. Anytime that something even so small such as a free coffee, a discount, or hitting all green lights I would express appreciation for knowing that everything in my reality now is because God placed it there, God allowed it. I started speaking to the Divine, not through prayer but through my own thoughts, and spoke to the Divine like I was speaking to my best friend. The more that I connected to God, the more I saw signs in my external reality that confirmed my beliefs and thoughts.

Being new to spirituality, I allowed myself to witness all kinds of perspectives and methods of connecting to God without judgment and slowly began forming my own practice, connection, and beliefs that feel authentic and genuine to me. The more that I was able to connect with God, the more that I was able to see myself through God's eyes, find my purpose, and develop confidence and self-trust in my own path and experience, knowing that I was being guided by the Divine and following the guidance. When God told me to heal, I did. When God told me to move, I did. When God told me to speak up, I did. When God told me to be still, I was. When God told me to wait, I did. When God told me to prepare, I did. Over time as I followed the guidance, I realized that I was cocreating my reality with God who was carving the path ahead for me. We just have to learn how to quiet the noise in order to hear clearly.

I began to build upon my foundation by addressing my fear of death for example by finding a new perspective. I now view death as a transition, as an ending that provides a new beginning. I no longer fear it as I have developed my connection to God and understand that we are energy, and energy cannot be created or destroyed, so I believe that our energy goes elsewhere after we leave our physical vessel. I restructured my view of heaven and hell which many believe are physical places. I believe we never left heaven; we are in heaven right now in this life, and we can choose to live in heaven on earth or create our own hell, consciously or unconsciously. Heaven to me is not a physical place, but a feeling of being connected to Source and seeing that reflected in our own reality. By allowing myself the space to explore new perspectives, I actually created a belief system that is so true to me that I can feel it in every fiber of my being, although it does not have to be the same for you. I would now like to share some aspects of my belief system for your free exploration, without any pressure or expectation of you to take it as fact, but to possibly invoke some internal conversations that you can begin to have with yourself.

Space and Time: Through studying quantum physics, I now understand that space and time are an illusion projected by our own consciousness, so I no longer look at time as a linear construct and space as a limited phenomenon, therefore my belief is that everything exists all at once and can be accessed in the present moment (you just have to adjust your frequency and subconscious to be able to access it). To put this into perspective (according to my belief system) there are multiple timelines occurring simultaneously. There is a timeline occurring right now where you are healthy, rich, fulfilled, and abundant, just as there is a timeline existing where you are overweight, sad, and working paycheck to paycheck. You can experience the timeline that you want in your physical reality by adjusting your frequency to the version of you living that timeline. This is essentially the work that I do by helping clients adjust their frequency and reprogram the subconscious so that they embody that desired frequency and therefore experience the corresponding effects in their reality.

We are all one, and we are all connected: We are all one, meaning that there is only one thing (Source consciousness, God) that exists and that everyone and everything is made out of that one thing because there is nothing else to make anything from. In short, the purpose of this human experience is to learn and grow. This learning and growing affects everyone; as you raise your frequency, you raise the frequency of the collective.

What goes around comes around: Everything is energy, and the more you radiate thoughts of love, kindness, and support, and the more you live in faith that everything is happening for your highest good, that energy will be reflected back to you. This also goes for undesirable outcomes that we can also manifest in a place of fear, doubt, and control. Remember that you cannot fake energy or intention, so if your intention is not in the right place God sees that. I experienced many blockages whenever I tried to create services or products solely for the money or out of desperation. God blocked these opportunities from coming to fruition because my intention was not aligned with my actions. This is the concept of karma and karma is not good or bad. Karma is the energy that you have put out into the field, the universe, or God that is reflected back to you.

While these do not constitute my whole belief system, these are a few major changes that I was able to switch on at the subconscious level so that it is second nature, and innate to me now. You do not have to agree with me or hold the same beliefs. The biggest thing that I have learned is to understand that beliefs and perspectives can change constantly. I've had plenty of people come forward telling me about their opinion on my belief system and even project their fear onto me because my guess is that hearing my differing beliefs is triggering to their own belief system. The difference between myself and them is that I am so wholeheartedly living from my truth that these comments no longer bother me and so in turn, I do not reciprocate that fear or shame them for their beliefs, even if they are different from mine. People may have something to say if you have different beliefs, but that does not mean you are wrong or need to conform. Let's hold space for each other to explore and express our beliefs, as I am sure that there are others that hold the same ones that you do.

Section 2.8—Integration and Expansion

As you can see, this book is titled *The Integrated Self* for a reason. Our message is in holistically removing the barriers that are preventing you from becoming your authentic self; the thoughts, beliefs, behaviors, and actions that are not aligned to your true frequency, who you naturally are. Integration is the solidifying of the new thought, perspective, belief, or feeling into the subconscious and the body to become an innate part of you. Think of integration as you teach a child colors. At first, they need to learn the color names and then experience matching the names to the colors. When you start quizzing them, they may not fully know, may be confused, and may not be 100 percent accurate every time. You know the child has integrated the colors when they can easily and confidently get those colors correct all of the time. Along this journey of growth, you will learn so many things about yourself but there is a difference between knowledge and wisdom. Knowledge is the knowing and understanding of these aspects of Self, whereas wisdom is gained when you apply the knowledge to an experience for both the mind and body to integrate the new way of being.

For example, when I was in between worlds per se, unlearning my old self and learning the new self, I had reprogrammed my subconscious thoughts to automatically think empowering thoughts of confidence, have a heightened belief in myself, and positive self-talk. At this time, I was learning to integrate this confidence into my mind and body, but I was neglecting the body aspect. I would think a new thought of self-confidence; however, my body responded with uneasiness, anxiety, and a little bit of fear. That is because while my mind was on board with the new identity, I hadn't practiced feeling into the body what this self-confidence feels like. This created incoherence between my mind and my body, where I knew I was growing and moving closer to the new self, but I was not allowing the body to feel into the new experience.

Once I began regulating my nervous system and pairing the new thought (intention) with the corresponding feeling and continued to practice that new way of being, I now have integrated this self-confidence. You know that you have integrated a lesson or a new aspect when it becomes second nature, innate, easy, and familiar to think, feel, or behave that way. Just because you practice a new thought once, does not mean it has been integrated. This is because the subconscious programming is stronger than your conscious mind, so you are essentially *overriding* the subconscious which is our innate programming with something new. This *overriding* then becomes the new subconscious programming once it has been integrated by embodying the beliefs, thoughts, feelings, and choices of the new program.

The Integrated Self is the version of you that has embraced and truly learned from past experiences (good or bad), released attachments, and is a pure expression of who you are without the conditions, expectations, and opinions of anyone else. A lot of people get into this work initially because they want to change their external reality such as manifesting material things like money or specific people. What a lot of people do not understand is that all that is required of you is to heal, to grow, to take accountability, and to be honest with yourself. We do not manifest what we want, we manifest who we are, what frequency we are embodying, and what experiences match our current beliefs, thoughts, feelings, and behaviors.

When we are first placed on this earth forgetting that we are of God, our memories are wiped of who we truly are in the ethereal, along with all the wisdom we held, the goal is to make the journey back to your natural frequency through these dense human conditions such as war, poverty, discrimination, and chaos that are set up to keep us from remembering. It is on purpose that we do not mention too much in this book about finding your purpose because ultimately, the purpose of your existence is to exist and to find that natural expression of yourself, your authentic self. Speaker and author Daryl Anka says,

> When you think of yourself as an indestructible external infinite being, nothing is ever really lost... Know thyself, be authentic, be your true self, live your true life, understand what it means to act on your passion because that is your magnetic compass needle pointing to your magnetic north. Know who you are, and live who you are because the most difficult thing is to actually try and be someone you are not.[13]

As I began my story in this part of this book, I mentioned spiritual awakenings and how many people are beginning to consciously remember that they are spiritual beings here living a human experience. Patrick and I believe it is very interesting that we are creating this book in a time where we see this happening all over the world, in addition to information being released about the true nature of our universe. Many people are starting to walk this path in their individual unique ways, and looking for guidance when it comes to balancing your humanness (personal identity, ego, inner critic), with your spirituality (soul, intuition, purpose).

In the next part, we will introduce the Model and how you can begin to self-reflect and evaluate. A couple of things to remember as we continue onto the Model and then read about Patrick's experience is that everyone has both light and dark within, that you hold the power to feel and create what you desire, and that in order to genuinely grow and evolve along this journey, you must be willing to look in the mirror and learn the things that are holding you back from embodying your authenticity and living the life you want to live.

If the Divine was just there to give us whatever we wanted without change or growth, there would be no evolution taking place, and no incentive to grow. God, the Universe, Source, is here to guide you through your journey of self-discovery and evolution as you return to your authentic frequency and begin living a life aligned with your beliefs and your truth. It is important to create balance for yourself along your journey as I had made that mistake myself and is partly my inspiration for this Model. When I had my first spiritual awakening, I was very much on the Soul side of the model where I was meditating, soul-searching, and visualizing, so much so that I created an imbalance between my spirituality and my humanness. I spent more time alone and realized that I was so imbalanced that I was ungrounding myself from the human experience. It felt weird to go out for drinks or to watch TV as my beliefs about life and the world at the time were being rebuilt.

This is your reminder that while it is admirable to grow, heal, and evolve, please do not forget that you are still human. You are here to exist, to experience, to love, to laugh. Try to make sure that you are taking care of your body, your mind, and your spirit on this journey of self-discovery. While there are times to draw our energy back and others when we are more social, you do not have to isolate yourself and then come out as this new person. Go out in the real world and practice what you've learned, experience yourself in new environments, new identities that feel aligned, and challenge yourself to learn from others.

Most importantly of all, spread love, spread your message, and share your creations and perspectives with an open heart, as the world needs your light. Those who are truly doing the spiritual work don't brag, step on people to get to the top, or make others feel less important or less evolved. As I said before, we are all one and everyone's on their own path, trajectory, and making their own choices. Be a walking expression of someone doing the work, and know that you cannot change anybody else. Who you are and what you do behind closed doors is what matters the most. So who are you? Who are you really?

PART 3

Overview of the Integrated Self Model

Section 3.1—Introduction to the Integrated Self Model

The essential key to understanding and maximizing the human-spirit experience is all about creating balance. It is about being centered in your body, mind, and spirit. It is about aligning to an equilibrium between the light and the dark to heal from childhood wounds and to survive failed relationships with as little struggle and angst as possible. When we are balanced and centered, we feel peace.

Dr. Wayne Dyer made it clear that he understood the importance of balance, as well as the struggle that existed and persisted in the human experience. Opening his book, *Being in Balance* with, "The concept of balance defines the universe. The cosmos, our planet, the seasons, water, wind, fire, and earth are in perfect balance. We humans are the only exception… [Dyer's book was his] attempt to help you restore this natural equilibrium in all aspects of your life."[14] In this particular book itself, Dyer was focused on the balance of desire and action: "Getting in balance is not so much about adopting new strategies to change your behaviors, as it is about realigning yourself in all of your thoughts so as to create a balance between what you desire and how you conduct your life on a daily basis."[15]

The Integrated Self Model explains how we can create balance between the mind through ego development, and the spirit through soul evolution. If you concentrate on one aspect, while neglecting the other, you experience an imbalance in your being (Self) and it creates a conflict within you, creating an internal confusion, an uneasiness of Spirit, and an incongruency of Self. The Integrated Self Model allows us to understand that these two aspects of Self (the human Ego and the Soul) exist and allow us to build comprehensive personal and spiritual growth strategies to rebalance these human Self aspects.

The balance between the Ego and Soul does not happen without conscious awareness. Instinctively, humans are preoccupied with the subjugation by their respective egos, and with the dramatic interactions with other like-minded, ego-minded humans, who are controlled by their own subconscious programming. This ego preoccupation typically extends through the teenage years and can actually remain prevalent through the end of life. So much of our early years is spent acting and reacting according to our egos, which are eagerly and energetically encouraged by our subconscious programming, primarily occurring between ages zero and seven years old.

Interpersonal interactions with other humans that are driven by the ego-mind are not always negative, not always aggressive, and not always unconscious; however, these programmed actions and reactions will always be self-serving, bent on survival, and focused on self-preservation using the well-known tactics of fight, flight, freeze, or fawn to keep the Self safe (or at least, as safe as possible at the moment). The ego will look for, or create opportunities to learn and to grow in ways that will elevate the status of the ego (within the parameters of its Self identity) in the mind of the ego (which lives mostly in the subconscious mind, though a partnership with the conscious mind may develop to varying degrees during life).

Balance of the Self tends to start with an initial and then ultimately growing sense of Soul awareness before an actual, fully conscious spiritual awakening occurs. This spiritual awakening that starts with soul awareness, just as with ego development, is iterative, unsteady, and nonlinear in nature. Once this spiritual growth reaches a critical mass relative to the ego development progression, people tend to focus primarily on this spiritual distraction; a distraction from a disappointing and unfulfilling life doing a litany of occupations and preoccupations, which in itself serve as distractions from the confusion, conflict, and struggle caused by the prevailing imbalance before the spiritual awakening began and could eventually take hold.

Once the imbalance between the Ego and Soul is being addressed through conscious work, attending to each of these human aspects, the human individual's level of consciousness will begin to take hold and expand (i.e., grow). Expanding consciousness is the process of moving toward higher levels of consciousness, higher levels of vibration, whether as an intentional seeker of enlightenment or only an aware, conscious (or unconscious) pedestrian in life experiencing the duality of the universe, from unconsciousness to enlightenment. Expanding consciousness, advancing through the Levels of Consciousness, can be enticing, even addictive, once a person pushes through the lower levels of consciousness, gains momentum, and experiences the high vibrations associated with the next level of consciousness.

As our consciousness or awareness of the *true* nature of this world and our *true* connection to The Divine grows, the connection of Ego and Soul increases. At the lower levels of consciousness, Ego and Soul are seen as the same with little or no individuation of the pieces. At the lower levels of consciousness, we may not even have a sense that we have a soul or that there is a God or Source of all things. As consciousness increases, we sense that we have an Ego and a Soul and we perceive them as separate, unconnected parts of the whole, which causes internal confusion and conflict. At the upper levels of consciousness, we understand the Ego and the Soul are both separate and connected, and together they are the whole of our Being.

Section 3.2—Origin of the Integrated Self Model

This section is not going to be what you expect! Normally when we learn how an invention or idea was created, it involves an inventor or free thinker who creates from scratch until the whole invention is completed. The origin of the Integrated Self Model is nothing like these processes but instead, a truly remarkable experience of an exchange of information between Patrick and the Divine.

The Integrated Self Model (formerly known as the Real Life Integrated Self Model) presented itself to Patrick in a very unusual way. On the morning of March 13, 2009, Patrick woke up earlier than normal with an unexplainable urge to get up. As he got out of bed, there was a rush of information flowing through him with the force of a firehose. Patrick felt the urge to pick up a notebook and start writing. If you know Patrick, you know that journaling is not something that comes naturally to him and is not an activity or exercise that he does often. Patrick didn't even journal or have a diary at the time, but he obediently began writing. He wrote anything and everything that was flowing to him, through him, and onto the pages of the notebook.

In addition to key words, main topic ideas, and references, Patrick sketched out diagrams with various geometric shapes until the vision of today's model slowly took form in the shape of a larger isosceles triangle, consisting of a trapezoid at the base and four smaller isosceles triangles stacked on top.

While Patrick has a degree in communication and a master's degree in counseling psychology and counselor education, he did not recognize the form and content of the model, not really. However, Patrick does remember observing the model on paper and connecting his real-life experiences to it. Essentially, the information he was receiving matched up with his personal and professional experience, but Patrick felt unsure about what the purpose of these documents was.

For about the next three months, Patrick expanded upon the notes and sketches from that morning, organizing them before formally documenting them with a public notary in May 2009. Once the model was notarized, Patrick put it away knowing that it was not the right time to expose the model. Patrick was just completing his master's degree in counseling and planning to open his private counseling practice as a registered psychotherapist. He began his career specializing in couples and family therapy and formed professional relationships as well as building his experience, reputation, and credibility on top of his formal education and life experience.

Due to personal challenges as well as the economic shift that began in 2008, Patrick closed his private therapy practice after three years to focus on his family and friends. Life went on, and Patrick continued his information technology (IT) career until 2022 when he was inspired to start his business back up offering life coaching support as a registered psychotherapist. Patrick wanted to help people with real-life issues, offering support from the perspective of both the physical and spiritual world.

In early November, Patrick started connecting with Arianna through social media on common topics of healing, mental health, as well as spirituality. When they met on a call they instantly aligned in values and beliefs, but also shared a lot of the same experiences in childhood as well as the present day. Patrick introduced Arianna to the Integrated Self Model who then began to study and reflect on Patrick's findings from years ago. Since Arianna comes from a background of holistic health, Arianna was not only fascinated by Patrick's ideas from years prior and resonated with the model in her personal life but also realized she could provide a whole new element to it.

The divine timing of this presentation and connection with Patrick baffled Arianna. She was in a time of her journey and professional career where she was struggling to connect spirituality with her healing work. When Patrick reached out and presented the model to her, she knew this was divinely orchestrated and guiding her to her purpose. It is exactly what she needed to bridge the gap between these two worlds; wellness and spirituality.

Patrick and Arianna began meeting weekly to discuss the model and how they could improve it with the intention of writing this book together. In between writing, they began exchanging client referrals because of their differing scopes of practice and approaches.

While Patrick is the *creator* of the Integrated Self Model, he knows without a doubt that the model was gifted to him through divine inspiration. The ultimate truth of it all is that the model was given to him in 2009 and he was guided through another spiritual awakening through divine intervention in 2022 to bring the model into the light and begin sharing it with the world.

Patrick respectfully and humbly considers himself the "spiritual custodian" of the Integrated Self Model and accepts his role in ensuring this model is presented to the world as a framework to better understand and evaluate one's growth in the human-spirit experience.

While the Integrated Self Model proves to be helpful as an evaluation tool for understanding the journey of evolution as a spiritual being living a human experience, it is important to note that this model is to be used as a tool and not to be considered black and white. We know that there are many ways, solutions, and frameworks that can be valid. This model and approach to the human-spirit experience will impact people in real-life situations in a positive way toward balanced growth. This model is not intended to replace therapists, coaches, or processes of such professionals. It is an orientation, a framework for consciously considering and approaching mental health in a more holistic way in combination with spiritual evolution.

Section 3.3—Overview of the Integrated Self Model

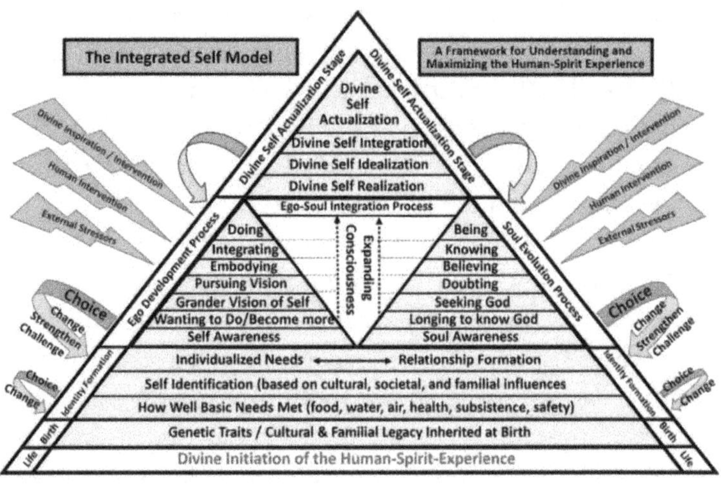

At first glance, the Integrated Self Model may seem overwhelming to comprehend. Our goal was to create something for anyone who is healing and evolving to use as a guide to orient themselves in their experience. Once we can pinpoint where we may lie on the model, we can ask ourselves some questions and evaluate the imbalance or area that needs attention to come back to balance. When our mind, body, and spirit are balanced, we can then expand with the least amount of resistance and be in a mode of energetic alignment and receptivity to our desires and new experiences.

The best way to introduce the Integrated Self Model is by starting with a high-level view of the different sections that comprise it. Each section has a primary premise and underlying questions to present the main focus of that section. We will review the main sections, and will later discuss the relationships between these sections so you can navigate the human-spirit adventure with the least amount of resistance on your journey. This model is to be used as a roadmap to view the uneven terrain and to masterfully navigate the challenges and opportunities of the physical 3D world.

Following are the two simplistic views of the model presenting their main sections along with their overarching questions. We will start with the high-level view at the base of the diagram, proceeding in a relative order up the model, though the actual experience through the model will be unique and dependent upon personal choice and divine intervention.

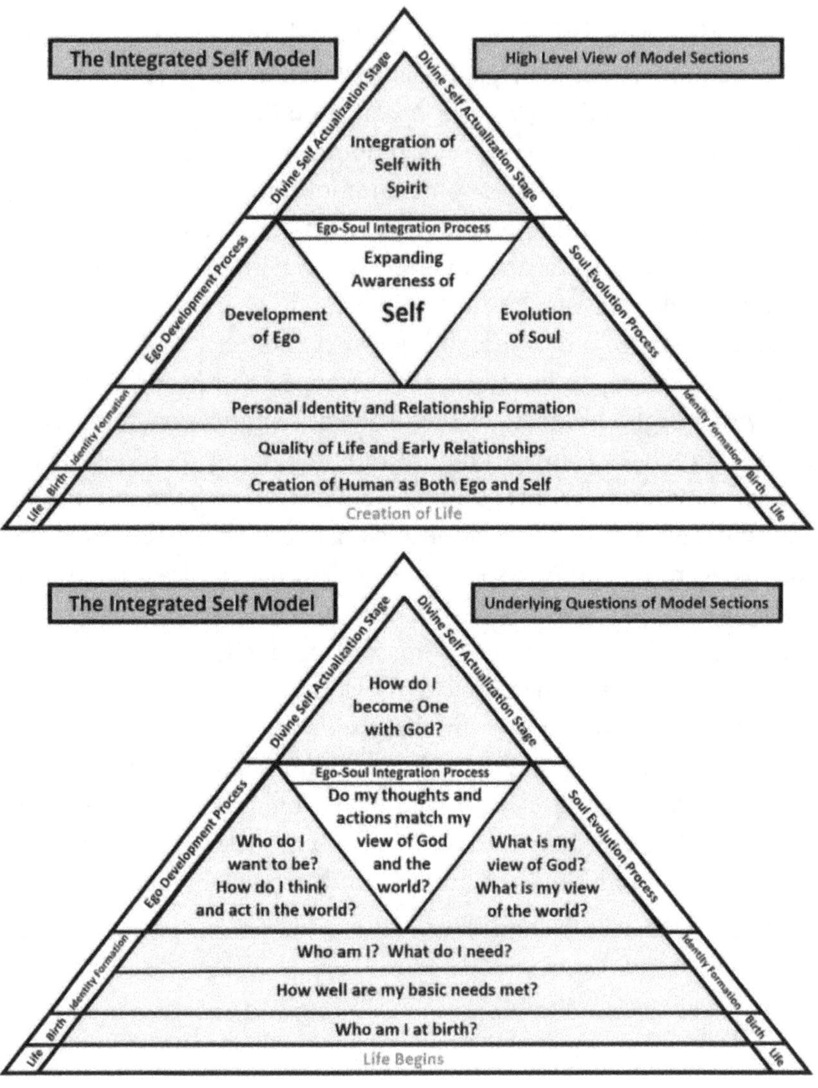

Section: Creation of Life
Underlying Question: How did you get here?
Where did you come from?

While there is no underlying question for this section on the model images, this section is meant to be a starting point of life creation. It is imperative that we each minimally have a story or idea, whether believed, imagined, contrived, or personally known without a doubt, of what comes before this human-spirit lifetime on earth and what comes after our time in this world at our ultimate conclusion. Whatever your belief of why, how, and when human life begins, we can at least all agree that we each have a beginning and end to this human-spirit experience. It is important for each of us to have a basic prevailing belief around the creation of human life; however, it is not imperative that we all have the same shared story or belief around this to effectively use the Integrated Self Model. It is also natural for your beliefs to change or expand throughout your experience, but having a belief system in place here provides a stable foundation for the other levels.

Section: Birth (Creation of Human Self as Both Ego and Soul)
Underlying Question: Who am I at birth?

Just as with the origination of life, and with the precise point when life begins for each human being born of this world, there is never just one accepted answer to this question of "who are we at birth?" Scientifically, it is widely agreed upon that the DNA provided by our biological parents, at least in part, contains physical characteristics and traits of our direct ancestors. It is even a widely accepted opinion that our DNA also includes some level of aptitude, skills, and behavioral characteristics of the blood-related generations that came before us.

In addition to the scientific-based answer to who we are at birth, the spiritual community holds the belief that God/Spirit blesses each person with spiritual gifts and a divine purpose to achieve during our human lifetime. Metaphysical belief systems that describe supernatural abilities and realities beyond the physical world offer whole new dimensions to this discussion, literally. Since each person's belief system is unique and personal, it is important to examine your belief system, including what you accept as truth, what you reject as false, and what you are not sure about quite yet.

Section: Identity Formation (Quality of Life and Early Relationships)

Underlying Question: How well were my basic needs met as a child (ages 0–7)?

We all have the same basic needs during our early childhood years to support human development from both a physical and mental perspective. These basic human needs include but are not limited to food, water, air, health, clothing, housing, safety, and love (having a consistent, nurturing caregiver). Unfortunately, most of us only partially receive these basic needs and then only to varying degrees of what is actually required during this critical childhood developmental stage.

Underlying Question: What was the quality of significant early relationships?

Early relationships are extremely important and influential to our childhood development in general and the development of healthy attachment behaviors, specifically. From birth until about the age of two years old, we require that our primary caregiver be extremely consistent, caring, and nurturing. For any secondary caregiver, it is essential that they provide a sense of normalcy in congruence with the primary caregiver, otherwise, the infant's sense of safety will be challenged, and attachment disorders may develop. A primary caregiver who struggles with mental health conditions and/or addictions will also tend to cause significant attachment disorders in the dependent children.

Typically, no person receives every basic need to a sufficient level required for healthy growth during this early childhood developmental stage to prevent mental health issues. Therefore, each person will carry at least some childhood issues from their early years into their adolescent, teen, and adult years. Depression, anxiety, and attachment disorders (to name only a few mental health issues) have become prevalent in our societies, and they persist throughout our lives unless significant, focused therapeutic work is undertaken for the mental health issues, specifically to bring about some degree of inner child healing. Many different approaches and kinds of therapy exist that have proven helpful in addressing and healing from childhood trauma as every person's journey is unique to them. These childhood issues play a significant role in the formation of our personal identities, including our personal challenges and struggles, throughout our respective lifetimes.

Section: Identity Formation (Personal Identity and Relationship Formation)
Underlying Question: Who am I? What is my personal identity?

Approximately at the age of twelve or thirteen years old, we each take on a personal identity (either passively or actively constructed) with the intended purpose of taking on and navigating the real world as an adult based on how we fit in society and the world.

The new personality formed at this stage can be an extension of our current personality traits and characteristics, supplementing identified areas of deficiency, and accepting our childhood issues (including but not limited to trauma, abuse, neglect, and attachment issues) as an integral part of our ongoing personality. The new personal identity construct can be a whole external facade to supplement, camouflage, and hide the existing personal identity that is considered significantly inadequate, deficient, flawed, and incapable of surviving, let alone thriving, in the 3D world.

During the teen years, we embody this either existing, constructed, or combined personality (whether conscious or not) and begin to receive feedback from others. We may take risks or act out of character to test, hone, embrace, or reject aspects of the chosen identity. We also observe our parental figures to see how they respond and navigate through situations and learn to take on the characteristics that will support our new identity while rejecting those personal traits that will not.

Underlying Question: What do I need from relationships? What do I need from the world?

Our experiences with our significant early relationships form the basis of the overall set of needs and expectations that we place on the relationships later developed during our lifetime. Initially, in the early stages of our lives, we seek out friendships that validate us or make us feel good. These early relationships tend to be about supplementing the basic relationship needs and support that were not received from our parents, family, and caregivers during our early childhood years.

During our teen and adult years, we seek out friendships and work experiences that validate our personal identity. As our personal identity changes through our choices, and also organically as a result of our personal growth and spiritual evolution, our existing relationships will naturally become strained, changed, or misaligned. This is why typically our friendships, jobs, and other relationships change over the course of our lifetime. Many times, we will take on a persona (personality construct) to fit in with a group of friends, a community, or even the world. Sometimes we may get lost in this persona for a while or even a lifetime if we do not become consciously aware of our Self and our Soul.

We tend to approach our romantic relationships differently than friendships. When we are looking for possible romantic partners, we are instinctively and unconsciously drawn to relationships that resemble our personal relationship with one of our parents. Most of the time, it is the parent from whom we did not get our basic needs met in the areas of nurturing, validation, affection, and/or love. We enter into these mostly unhealthy relationships with the intent to work toward and finally receive the validation and love that we did not get from our parents.

If you were fortunate enough to have had a validating, nurturing, loving relationship with your parents during your early childhood developmental years, or if you worked on your mental health issues as an adult, you may have an opportunity for healthier adult relationships; that is if your partner is at the same or similar point of dealing with childhood issues in a healthy manner as you are.

Section: Ego Development Process (Development of Ego)
Underlying Question: Who do I want to be?
How do I think and act in the world?

The process of ego development basically starts when the individual enters or prepares to enter the adult world of self-sufficiency, self-preservation, and some level of expected productivity. Although the ego development process can overlap considerably with the later teen-years, it really begins once the individual experiences separation or emancipation from the core family system. Based on our personal identification of who we really are and who we want to present ourselves as to the world, we must choose a personal identity; a set of personal characteristics to present to others as who we are now and who we are going to be in the world.

Through this personal identity, we move through the world forming a belief system from a perspective of validation, relationship, and safety. We continually assess whether the persona or identity that we have created is working in the world to (1) earn a minimal level of validation to support the Ego's sense of self, (2) have adequate resources to establish a safe home and work life, and (3) build relationships that foster the sense of belonging through community, friendships, and relationships.

Besides working to know who we are in this world, we also come to instinctively form a belief system about the world itself for our own self-protection. As we walk through life, we determine if the world itself is safe and supportive of our personal identity, or if the world is dangerous and threatening to us and our lifestyle. Through this lens of danger and protection, we form a belief about our control over life and our circumstances. We may feel as though we are personally controlling what happens in our lives or begin to wonder if there is an influence, a power, outside ourselves that influences what happens.

The belief system that we form about people and the world around us will capture the primary concerns and considerations that will influence our motivation to stay the same or change. In the normal course of living, there are plenty of opportunities for change that can be triggered by human intervention, divine intervention, or divine inspiration. Without any motivation or incentive, we would choose to stay unchanged and safe, in a state of homeostasis, comfortability, and the known. Without motivation, choice, and change, we would not truly be living in the world, and the human-spirit experience would not be much of an experience at all.

Section: Soul-Evolution Process (Evolution of the Soul)
Underlying Question: What is my view of God?
What is my view of the world?

The process of soul evolution typically will start once the ego development process has progressed to a point when the ego's identity is fairly set and stable enough so that the ego is feeling relatively safe (or at least not threatened in a life-or-death manner). At this point, some life event experienced by the human Ego will trigger something in the human Soul to begin to awaken. The human Self becomes aware of the Soul, aware that there is something unseen to be experienced. This triggering event that causes the Soul to awaken typically occurs from an act of divine inspiration or intervention, though human intervention could provide the needed spark to initiate the awareness of the human Soul.

Prior to the actual awakening of the Soul, our view of the world has been formed by the Ego and comprises our personal belief system. Much of our belief system, especially initially, comes from our core family, friends, community, and the society in which we live. As the Soul awakens, the Soul compares its own experiences from a spiritual perspective with the belief system already formed by the Ego. The more that the Soul remembers, the stronger the influence of God/Spirit will have on the experiences of the human Soul.

As with the belief system that is formed by the Ego about the physical 3D world, the Soul forms its beliefs about the spiritual world from its own soulful perspectives and experiences. As the individual components of the Ego's belief system are examined from the Soul's perspective and compared with the growing awareness of God/Spirit, the imbalance between the Ego and the Soul will fluctuate. The imbalance may favor one side or the other during different phases in the human-spirit lifetime working toward balance until such a time where the Ego and Soul enter into a conscious partnership, working toward the mutual good of both. When the Ego and Soul are in balance, we are able to maximize and expand our energy, evolve more quickly, and even connect with the divine at deeper, more subtle levels.

As with the Ego's relationship with choice and change, the Soul will have opportunities to make choices to change its own set of beliefs (or not) during the normal course of being in the 3D world. However, these opportunities will be primarily triggered by divine inspiration, divine intervention, or human intervention. The main difference here is that the Soul will continue to seek God/Spirit without any motivation from the 3D world as the Soul awakens fully through the evolution process. However, if the Ego's experiences become stressed or strained enough, the Soul's evolution may be accelerated and the imbalance of influence on the human Self will shift to the Soul, and it will remain with the Soul unless/until the Ego development improves. The Ego will tend to remain a strong influence in the human-spirit experience as long as the Ego makes choices for its highest good and eventually establishes a joint partnership with the Soul.

Section: Divine Self-Integration Process
(Integration of Self with Spirit)
Underlying Question: How do I become one with God?

The process of Divine Self Integration is to be considered the road less traveled in the model. The human-spirit Self tends to operate within the middle and lower levels of the Model. When a high level of consciousness is realized, the Ego and Soul have fully integrated this new vibration and perspective. The ultimate goal of this path is to rejoin God/the Divine and be one with God once again spiritually, if not literally, when we leave this physical 3D world.

The human-spirit Integrated Self may be attracted to enter this stage because the expansion of consciousness can become quite addictive. The ease of life and peace that come with the higher levels of consciousness can open the Integrated Self to the possibility of even higher levels and greater peace. There are infinite possibilities that are available to us, we just have to tap into, observe, and embody those frequencies. The possibility of being even closer to God/Spirit can entice the human-spirit Self to continue its relative ascent by way of enlightenment.

Section 3.4—Lifecycle of the Human-Spirit Self

The best way to become familiar with the Integrated Self Model is to view it as the lifecycle of the human-spirit self (ego and soul) during this single lifetime in this 3D world. The lifecycle of the human-spirit self (which can be laid over the model) has the following components; some of which are sequential steps, and some of which are iterative in nature; all driven by the influence of choice, change, intervention, and/or inspiration.

Just as with the model, we have two variations of the lifecycle to observe; one showing the general framework (higher level), and the other going deeper into specific steps (lower level). Immediately when looking at the higher-level view of the model, we notice that the lifecycle begins with incarnation. You will also notice that the left side of the lifecycle portrays the masculine energy of doing, which also lines up with the left side of the model, the Ego. The right side of the lifecycle shows the feminine energy of being, which is our Soul side of the model.

Just as in the model where we discussed how at different points in life you may fall out of balance toward one side, the same persists in the lifecycle with doing and being. Sometimes life requires more work and more energy for us to give, and other times life slows down when we get the opportunity to embody the feminine energy of being.

The Lifecycle of the Human-Spirit Self

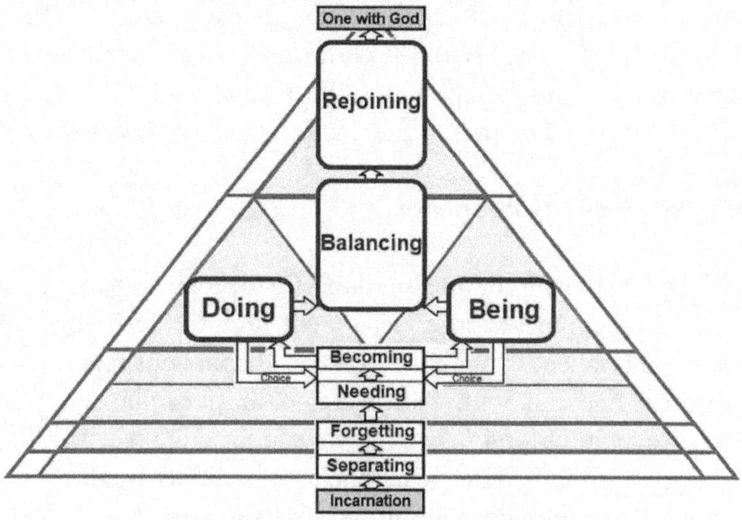

The Lifecycle of the Human-Spirit Self

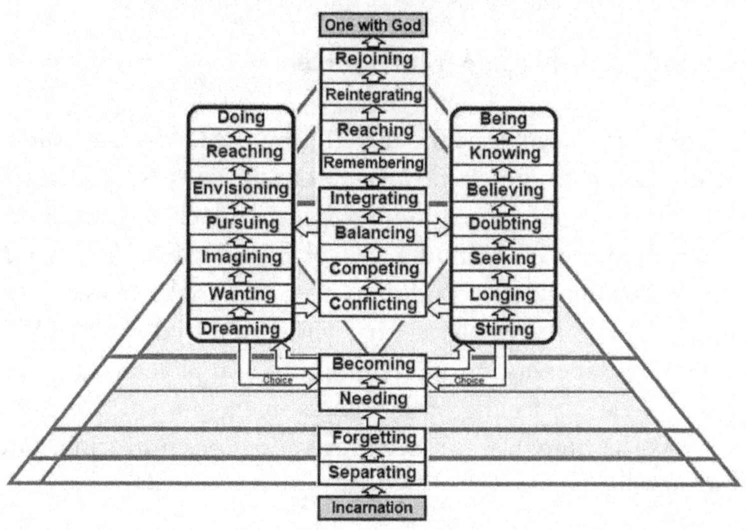

Incarnation (by God/Spirit):

As the entry point to the model and into this 3D world, an image of the Divine Self is created as the human Soul, the essence of your spirit. The human Ego is then created in contrast to the human Soul to provide a truly dynamic human-spirit experience for the Divine to know itself experientially. As the final part of incarnation, the human Soul is joined with the human Ego as the divine creation of the Human-Self. Through this incarnation, the human-spirit experience is initiated in a real way into the physical 3D world.

Separating (from God/Spirit):

At the moment of incarnation, we become separated from Source (although never truly separated) and the feeling of angst appears instantaneously with the initially unconscious space residing between the Ego and Soul. This feeling of angst can be described as the intense longing for a *home* that we cannot quite recall and for a *place* that we cannot quite remember. This results in an energetic undercurrent of longing, tension, and persistently anxious feelings rooted in separation anxiety (for the lack of a better term).

Forgetting (that we come from Source):

The separation of the human Self from the Divine Self is immediately and deeply submersed through the divine spell of forgetting. At this very moment, the angst of separation is locked within unconsciousness and locked behind a veil of illusions in a 3D world of drama, distractions, and conditions that will make it improbable, if not impossible to remember that you come from Source/Spirit/God without experiencing pain, suffering and/or loss. This act of forgetting creates a feeling of emptiness in the human Self that, in turn, feeds the human Ego's need for validation, nurturing, safety, and belonging.

Needing (validation and love):

As explained above, the human Ego is subconsciously driven to require and experience specific, preprogrammed needs during its lifetime, especially in the early childhood years. If we do not fulfill these needs, the Ego experiences stress, anxiety, depression, or the like. If the significant needs of the Ego are not satisfied sufficiently to provide a sense of contentment, belonging, and safety, some form of physical stress or internal conflict will be experienced, resulting in psychological (mental health) issues or physiological (physical health) issues. The greater the failure to gain safety, acceptance, and love in the world, the more severe, problematic, and chronic the trauma will be within the human Self.

Becoming (more in the 3D world):

At this point, the need for belonging, validation, and safety will tend to motivate the human Ego throughout this lifetime toward fulfilling this mission of finding and securing a sense (or illusion) of validation, belonging, and safety. The human Ego creates a personal identity, a persona, that will be used to construct a human Self that will be able to survive and even thrive during this lifetime. At this point, the human Ego is already preprogrammed to create an identity that provides a sense of safety (control) and that can attract relationships for validation, belonging, or procreation.

Doing (more in the 3D world):

In this process, the focus of the human Ego is on doing more in a focused, deliberate effort to attract more validation, a higher status, fulfilling relationships, and more resources to improve and continue this sense of safety of the human Self.

Dreaming: From very early in the lifecycle, the human Ego will start dreaming of the future, envisioning itself doing things, and experiencing the 3D world in ways that will elevate the Ego such as rewards, status changes, and a stronger safety net. Organically, the human Ego will have recurring daydreams and night dreams in which the human Ego will *dream* of *doing* things.

Wanting: Once the human Ego starts to dream, the specific dreams of itself "doing" things in various situations will naturally change and morph until one or more particular situational experiences begin to take hold and gain the favor of the Ego. At that point, the Ego starts wanting this experience as an expression or extension of its current identity, or even as an alternative to its current identity. This *wanting* becomes the motivation of the human Ego for choice, change, and moving toward self-actualization.

Imagining: Once one or more particular dreams have become a *wanting* within the human Ego, the dreams will increase in detail, allowing the human Ego to get a better idea of what this imaginary dream may look and feel like. In this step, the dream of doing something becomes a vague possibility but is not actually seen yet as a real possibility. This is the process of mentally experiencing the dream before actualizing it in this 3D world.

Pursuing: Continued dreaming about the vague possibility adds more and more detail to the imagined experience until it becomes a real possibility. The human Ego begins planning and taking real steps toward realizing this new experience, which will become the new or enhanced identity of Self. The human Ego is now pursuing the imagined experience in real-life ways. This is known as taking inspired action; using the breadcrumbs in our subconscious to create it in our reality.

Envisioning: As the now pursued dream moves from being vaguely possible to being actually possible with real steps taken toward the new personal identity, the Ego inserts increasingly more detail into the visions and begins envisioning itself in real-life situations for this pursued experience in order to gain a sense of actually being in that experience.

Reaching: Through the consistent planning, pursuing, and envisioning of this now very real possibility, the human Self approaches the realization of this held dream, by actually reaching this envisioned experience at the same time/space in the 3D world as it now occupies the human Self.

Doing: Upon reaching this goal and actually performing this new identity, the human Ego briefly settles into this new situation; however, it does not rest. The Ego instinctively continues to scan the landscape of the always threatening, always unsafe, 3D world and to assess ways to improve its current situation in terms of validation, belonging, and safety.

Being (more in the 3D world):

In this stage of the Human-Spirit lifecycle, the focus of the human Soul is on connecting with Source through peaceful existence and just being. The human Soul is not concerned with doing more (as is the human Ego) but rather being in a constant state of connection with Source. However, in the higher level of Ego and Soul integration, the Soul will allow the Ego to do more as long as the doing of the Ego is in alignment with the being of the Soul.

Stirring: At some point in the lifecycle, the human Ego will grow to a point at which it has developed and feels safe enough to unknowingly start allowing space for the Soul to emerge from the shadow Self. This emergence of the human Soul starts with a sense of missing something, the sense of forgetting something. The human Soul's awakening starts as a stirring that feels like a sense of beingness without any understanding of the reason or purpose. Once this stirring has started for the human Soul, it will continue to intensify, and the awakening of the Soul will persist.

Longing: Once the stirring of the Soul grows strong enough, a sense of longing begins to develop. This longing is rather abstract in nature, with the Soul not knowing for what it is longing. Nonetheless, the stirring morphs into a longing, a yearning, that will continue to grow and nag at the Soul until there is a subconscious call-to-action to move toward the sense of being in peace; and thus, moving toward Soul actualization while still operating in this 3D world.

Seeking: Once the call-to-action has been issued, the human Soul begins actively seeking the still unseen, unknown "Source" of the intense longing (i.e., Source). The human Self will first casually and then aggressively seek the Source, following the trail of breadcrumbs farther and farther in the physical 3D world looking for clues and then evidence until the Source begins to take on a spiritual form that is somewhat familiar, even familial, to the human Soul. In this step, the existence of Source becomes a hopeful possibility, but not actually believed yet as a real possibility.

Doubting: As the longing and seeking for the Source continues for an extended period of time, the target of the search becomes more and more formed in the spiritual mind of the human Soul. Because of the lack of physical evidence or proof that the Source of the longing actually exists, the human Soul finds its Self doubting the existence of the Source and then even doubting its own uncertain feelings of longing for something that does not seem to really exist. Even while doubting the existence of Source, the human Soul continues seeking the Source of the longing in earnest, all the while being frustrated and desperate to locate some bit of evidence.

Believing: Through the seeking of Source while doubting, the little bits of evidence that were originally missed or doubted begin to be realized and eventually add up to an undeniable level of proof that the Source of the longing, the source of Self, does really exist. The majority of this evidence is received in the form of a feeling, synchronicity, or undeniable events that allude to an unseen influence playing a role in the human-spirit experience. There is a moment, an instant, when the doubting is transformed into believing; that is, believing that there is a Source beyond this physical reality, a Source of the human Soul. Now the human Soul believes that it has always known Source, but it had forgotten its own divine origination.

Knowing: In this stage, proof of God/Spirit as the Source of the human Soul continues to mount, and momentum increases until a threshold of knowing is reached and surpassed. This knowing occurs when the human Soul releases all need for evidence or proof; no longer entertaining doubt or disbelief in the slightest. There are no longer any lingering questions to answer, no doubts to quiet, and no disbeliefs to resolve. There is only knowing now that it, the human Soul, was placed here in this world by Source. Once you know this, there is no not knowing or unknowing (i.e., forgetting) ever again. Even during the Ego states of anxiety, depression, disbelief, or despair, the Soul cannot forget that the Source of the human Soul, the Source of the human Self, is God/Spirit.

Being: Having gone through the angst of separation from Source, and through the lonely journey of forgetting, longing, doubting, seeking, and believing, the human Soul has now finally reconnected with its Source, with Source. Upon reaching its goal of remembering and reconnecting with Source while in the 3D world, the human Soul can now focus on just being; being connected to Source, being a soulful balance to the Doing of the human Ego for the possibility of realizing a more joyful, loving, peaceful human-spirit experience.

Balancing (Ego and Soul with expanding consciousness):

It is in this space between the Ego and the Soul where consciousness energetically resides in the human Self. At the beginning of the human-spirit lifecycle, the imbalance between the Ego and the Soul is naturally at its greatest. As the Ego develops and the Soul remembers, and as they become more in balance, consciousness will expand (i.e., increase) relative to the level of consciousness (see Section 5.8 Assess your Level of Consciousness) being experienced by the human Self.

Conflicting (between Ego and Soul): In this Model, the lower state of imbalance between the Ego and the Soul is referred to as internal conflict. This sense of conflict may present itself as a range of symptoms, such as anxiety, depression, physical ailments, confusion, and a sense of feeling lost (or similar), depending on the relative level of imbalance and on the work being done to consciously reduce the imbalance. At the beginning of life, the human Self is largely unconscious, and the Ego is unaware that the Soul even exists. Balance is not even considered at this stage.

Competing (between doing and being): Once the Ego and the Soul become sufficiently active, the lower state of imbalance changes from conflicting to competing with each other for control or influence of the human Self. The Ego and the Soul each have their own agenda, their own focus or path for navigating through the human-spirit lifecycle. This state of competing between the Ego and the Soul may present itself as a range of symptoms such as internal confusion, uneasiness, and stress (to name a few examples), and will be largely dependent on the degree of imbalance and the focused work being done to consciously reduce the imbalance and obtain or regain balance.

Balancing (Ego and Soul): In this stage of personal and spiritual growth, the Ego and Soul are each rowing individually and both starting to work toward establishing an equilibrium, a homeostasis, for moving through the human-spirit lifecycle in harmony. This balancing effort tends to be unconscious in the beginning and is initiated by a spark of consciousness usually at some point after the human Self has been focused on developing the Ego to a sufficiently safe level. This allows the echo of the Soul some space to come out of hiding and begin to awaken into the light. From this point, a relationship will be forged between the Ego and the Soul to work toward elevating the human Self and create mutually beneficial opportunities for both doing and being.

Integrating (Ego and Soul): During this process of integrating the Ego and Soul, the level of consciousness is increasing for the human Self, and both the Ego and Soul are working in partnership, in collaboration, toward a mutual goal. The separateness of Ego and Soul is minimized to a point where the separateness of the Ego and Soul has all but vanished, with both existing and each with its own equally important role to play. Through this partnership and collaboration of the human Ego and the human Soul, a divine purpose is designed, architected, or realized...one that will equally support the Ego and the Soul during its remaining days in this lifetime. At the highest point of the Ego-Soul integration process, the human Self is said to be both Self Actualized and Soul Actualized. The level of consciousness is also highly expanded to a consistent state of peace.

Rejoining (God and Integration of Self with Spirit):

Once consciousness has expanded and has experience living in a consistent state of peace (i.e., at a relative level of consciousness of 600+), the Integrated Self is presented with the possibility of moving even closer to Source through Enlightenment (level 700 and above). The fully Integrated Self must then consider if working through the divine self-integration process is desired, and then must consciously choose to go down that path, or not.

Remembering (we came from Source): In this stage, the Integrated Self experiences a sort of stirring, similar to what was felt at the start of the Soul Awakening stage. The Integrated Self begins remembering that not only is it connected to Source but also came from Source, as a part of Source. The Integrated Self then remembers clearly that it is directly connected with Source, and is actually part of the Divine.

Reaching (for Source): At this point, the Integrated Self begins reaching for Source, consciously working on expanding consciousness and moving toward full enlightenment. The human Self may read, study, learn, and connect with other people aligned with their level of consciousness all the while creating daily practices of self-reflection, contemplation, and meditation becoming the major focus.

Reintegrating (with Source): As the Integrated Self continues to increase its connection blissfully and consciously with Source, the level of consciousness continues to expand until the divine integration process is activated, and the Integrated Self begins to reintegrate with the Divine. The separation between Source and Self continues to evaporate until it has all but vanished. The Integrated Self perceives that there is no separation between itself and the Divine.

Rejoining (Source): Any remaining sense of separation, real or perceived disappears and the Divine Self/Soul Integration process of rejoining the Soul and Divine Self with Source has been completed.

One with Source:

At the point of exit out of the Integrated Self Model, leaving the human-spirit experience and the physical 3D world behind, the Divine Self containing the evolved human Soul ultimately returns once again as One with the Divine.

Section 3.5—Balance of the Ego-Soul Growth

As introduced previously, the Integrated Self Model is all about cultivating the balance between the ego (mind) development and the soul (spirit) evolution. If you concentrate on one aspect while neglecting the other, you experience an imbalance in your Self, which reveals itself as an internal confusion, uneasiness, and incongruency, without your knowing why and what to do to regain balance and reestablish the integrity of the mind and soul. This is also the feeling of when we hear people say, "I don't feel like myself." It is a disconnection, an incongruency between what the subconscious mind believes to be true, and what your Soul (your true being) is calling you toward. The greater the imbalance, the greater the internal confusion and conflict.

An imbalance can occur when you only focus on one aspect and neglect the other (whether consciously or unconsciously). The model allows us to understand that these two aspects of Self exist, the human Ego and the human Soul, and the model allows us to build personal and spiritual growth strategies to rebalance these human Self aspects. It is important to know that these imbalances are a normal part of the human-spirit experience. Through choices that support growth, we have opportunities to work toward balancing the Ego and human Soul.

The balance of the ego and soul does not just happen without conscious awareness and effort. Many focus on the ego development side by pursuing mental health initiatives such as mindset reprogramming, exploring the conscious and subconscious minds, and inner child healing, while others focus on the spiritual side through the practice of meditation, soul-searching, acquiring knowledge about energy, and manifestation. Without conscious awareness, there is little attention paid to both aspects of the human-spirit experience, especially not at the same time. This leaves each human being with a significant imbalance of Ego and Soul resulting in feelings of confusion or conflict,

> If this essential core (inner nature) of the person is frustrated, denied, or suppressed, sickness results, sometimes in obvious forms, sometimes in subtle and devious forms, sometimes immediately, sometimes later. These psycholog-

> ical illnesses include more than those psychological illnesses listed by the American Psychiatric Association... That is, general-illness of the personality is seen as any falling short of growth, or of self-actualization, or of full-humanness. And the main source of illness (although not the only one) is seen as frustrations (of the basic needs...) especially in the early years of life.[16]

The Ego Development (Actualization) Process first begins with a tenuous childhood experience that is mildly damaging at best or severely traumatizing at worst. This is the foundation from which we build our personal identity, develop unhealthy or inconsistent relationships, and an uncertain awareness of Self. The Soul Evolution (Actualization) Process starts with soul awareness at some point during human life, with the hope that it will happen earlier in life rather than later, if at all. Both the Ego-Development and the Soul Evolution processes are nonlinear and iterative in nature where neither process is guaranteed to even start, and not guaranteed to advance through completion (actualization) during one human lifetime.

The personal development and spiritual growth related to the Ego Development and the Soul Evolution processes are realized through hardship, pain, sorrow, grief, and conscious work. Spiritual Teacher Brittany Bento recently explained that "as hard as it is, hard times are beautiful. They're beautiful because that is where the majority of soul growth happens; that is where the majority of growth happens in general."[17]

The low vibrations and lower levels of consciousness are difficult, uncomfortable, and even painful but that is what allows us to experience higher levels of consciousness and vibration as it represents just one example of duality in this world. Without hardship, challenges, struggle, and mistakes there is no incentive to grow, nothing pushing us to heal, and nothing that is making us feel uncomfortable, which is the catalyst for change and experience outside the comfort zone. If you come to understand and accept that hardship and challenges bring the gift of opportunity for growth, you will also come to understand and believe that the hard times and challenges of human existence are gifts to be used to activate personal growth and spiritual remembrance by learning to use these opportunities for growth strategically and enthusiastically through the programmed resistance of the nature of the human Ego.

Before we awaken spiritually, we may choose to focus on our ego development by "doing better" and "doing more," which is a primary part of ego identity. This is driven by our unfulfilled needs as children to be loved and valued. With conscious work, we can concentrate on healing from the expectations and wounds inflicted by our unconscious and unintentional parents through inner child healing. With conscious personal mental health work, we can take that need to be loved and valued and turn it into superpowers of self-love and self-worth. Once we are no longer being driven to do more and be better based on our childhood needs to be loved and valued, our ego becomes less conflicted and less combative, becoming more cooperative and willing to experience new opportunities for growth.

Once the soul begins to awaken, the spiritual evolution tends to take on an energy, a light, of its own to keep the soul moving toward Source through a need to want to know more about the spiritual nature of the human-spirit experience. This soul evolution and spiritual growth will continue until the ego causes resistance because it is being neglected or ignored. This is the time when you must become intentional about your personal and spiritual growth to cultivate balance between the Ego and Soul. Once the soul begins to evolve and spirituality (faith) strengthens to match the ego, this is when you get to start "being more" in life and stop "doing" constantly so you can experience Source. Peace becomes a possibility once your soul begins to develop to such a degree that the ego is no longer in absolute control of your human-spirit experience and you are providing space for spirituality to blossom. Peace is experienced when you find a balance between the human Ego and the Soul.

When the Ego is no longer worried about being ignored or left behind and it has evolved through ego development, the ego is content in just doing things. It no longer feels driven by childhood issues, and no longer feels the need to keep you safe all of the time. When balance between the Ego and the Soul is achieved, your level of consciousness is raised, which allows the Ego and Soul to begin integration organically.

The intention of this model and book is to emphasize the significance of the integration of the Ego and Soul, which is a partnership and level of trust between these two aspects that brings the opportunity to experience true peace. If you have one aspect directing your thoughts and behavior without the other's input, this imbalance can result in resistance in the form of internal conflict, confusion, frustration, stress, hopelessness, or despair. In short, without balance of the Ego and Soul, mental health issues can persist and worsen along with physical ailments.

In many cases, the feeling by the Ego when it is ignored is the very thing that causes the Ego to declare, "Wait, you need me to keep you safe," just as the feeling by the Soul of never being brought into the light is the very thing that causes the Soul to awaken and proclaim, "Wait a minute, you need me to help you find peace." In the human experience, we need both; we need the human Ego to be in the physical world doing things masterfully and navigating a dangerous world in a way that keeps the human Soul safe so that the Soul can awaken, evolve, and move closer to Source together. Both the light (soul) and the dark (ego) can move closer to Source together in balance, which is where they integrate together. The more in balance you are with your ego and soul developments, the better integration happens and the better your experience of life becomes. Your internal confusion begins to settle and inner conflict begins to dissipate, and you are now able to move through life and up to higher levels of consciousness if that's what you choose to do. Remember, there is no one level of consciousness better than another; each level of consciousness provides a different, unique experience.

If you have a belief system that leads you to believe that you are going to get another chance at life in this world through reincarnation, soul assignment, or some other form of human life invocation, then maybe you are satisfied with being where you are in this lifetime, staying at the level of consciousness that provides you love and peace. Perhaps you believe that you have been through enough this time around and now your purpose is to just rest and experience what you'd like before your next human-spirit iteration in the 3D world. Maybe you believe your purpose is to help others relax or heal not by doing, but just by being your caring, loving self. Possibly, you want to discover or remember your life purpose and develop a practice of being and doing at the same time. Whatever your belief system holds for your human-spirit experience in this world, having your ego and soul in balance will provide you with the contentment, congruency, calmness, and peace within so that you may live your life empowered with the skills to beautifully handle obstacles and things out of our control.

This balance and integration of the Ego and Soul bring higher levels of energy, vibration, and corresponding advancements through levels of consciousness. This is where we can understand how the levels of consciousness directly affect the level of vibration. We can then use our awareness of Self, both the Ego and Soul, to manage emotional states of being, and therefore manage our level of consciousness and vibration. We will cover levels of consciousness and vibration later in this book.

Once you have fully developed your Ego through an iteration of challenge, choice, growth, and identity reformation, you will have completed your ego development. This is what Maslow called self-actualization in his Hierarchy of Needs theory. In the Integrated Self Model, we honor that contribution by Maslow, and at the top of the ego development process is self-actualization, and in kind, at the top of the soul evolution process is "soul actualization." A high level of consciousness of Self is experienced when both aspects are actualized, at which point you begin focusing more on Source and moving toward rejoining the Divine (if you choose) by becoming aware of the Divine Self within you. This brings an insatiable desire to be closer to Source which occurs at the top level of the Integrated Self Model pyramid, with the ultimate goal of being Divine Self actualized, and fully integrated back with the Divine as the Divine Self.

Section 3.6—Foundational Concepts and Pillars of the Model

The basic premise of the Integrated Self Model is that challenges in life are natural and normal as part of the human experience. Hardships and challenges encourage movement and growth as we are drawn toward reconnection and reintegration with Source. This does not take away from the weight and heaviness of these struggles or discount any experience, but it provides a perspective that challenges in life are the ultimate catalyst for growth. During our lives, we have struggles and imbalances between our Ego and Soul that cause considerable stress, struggle, and obstacles all bringing us toward a reconnection and reintegration with Source.

The scope of this model and framework is only the human experience from birth through the transition back to the Divine by the death of the physical body. The purpose of this model is not to explain the possible existence of past or future lives through reincarnation, nor is its purpose to describe or acknowledge any spiritual or metaphysical connections beyond this physical manifestation. However, the purpose is also not to discount, deny, or reject the possible reality of reincarnation, metaphysical connections, or other dimensions. These may be explored at a further date as complementary to this model but is not within the current scope of the Integrated Self Model.

It is an assumption of the model that represents the human-spirit experience, that mental health conditions and disorders will impact the effectiveness of people's abilities to move through life. These mental health challenges may cause temporary setbacks, stagnancy, or permanent disengagement from this model if the mental health conditions are not addressed. A person's mental health condition must be assessed to understand how disconnected the person is from this model and how to address the mental health condition effectively to help the person fully engage with this model.

The model is not a psychotherapy process and is not intended to replace therapeutic counseling and life coaching. It is intended to provide a framework from which to work during counseling and coaching in order to better understand the dimensions of a person's life and where they are out of balance along their journey of growth and evolution.

While it is not imperative that you accept the foundational concepts underlying the development of the Integrated Self Model for it to be valid and useful to you, it is important that you understand these concepts as a way to understand the absolute respect we have for the human experience, and that there is no one person or belief system that is better than another.

The foundational pillars of the Integrated Self Model are:

1. We are spiritual beings having a human experience.
2. We consist of and exist as both human Ego and human Soul, and both are equally important to and an integral part of our human-spirit experience.
3. The Ego and the Soul are manifestations/creations of Spirit as the human Self.
4. Life is a series of choices, and we define ourselves (our personal identities as Ego and Soul) by the choices we make.
5. We strengthen, challenge, or change our personal identities with each and every choice we make.
6. We create/select a new identity when a threshold of supporting choices is reached.
7. Opportunities for choice and change are presented through our chosen human experiences, human intervention, Divine Intervention, and Divine Inspiration.
8. Our Level of Consciousness of Source (The Divine) and the human experience directly affects our human perception of stress, struggle, conflict, and angst.
9. We strive for Ego Actualization and Soul Actualization, which are dynamic, incremental, constant, and ever-changing expressions of Self through our choices.
10. Ego Actualization and Soul Actualization may occur simultaneously and progress at different rates; however, we may choose to focus on one or the other or both at times.

11. The Ego must be balanced and integrated with The Soul (as the holistic expression of Self) to reduce stress and struggle and maximize the human-spirit experience.
12. Our ultimate goal is for Divine Actualization; that is, to rejoin or reintegrate with The Divine. Most of us only achieve this through physical death in this lifetime.

Section 3.7—Influence of Maslow's Hierarchy of Needs

When Patrick was first exposed to Maslow's Hierarchy of Needs theory many years ago, he recalls feeling relieved to find something that explains why he was the way he was. Patrick understood that he was a version of *normal* and that maybe there was a place for him in the world. For a moment, he had a sense of belonging and not merely existing as a one-off human being, lonely and alone.

Since a young child, Patrick has been very curious about the role of science (especially laws of physics such as the law of cause and effect) in his life, in the world, and in the universe. This interest in science was equaled, if not overshadowed by his curiosity and interest in the role of God (and therefore spirituality) in the world.

Patrick grew up in a Catholic family (much like Arianna) and attended Catholic schools followed by a Jesuit college and university. Even with extremely constant and focused religious influence, Patrick did not buy into God as a singular external locus of control on his life and the world around him. Even before the age of seven, Patrick could not accept God as a punishing entity, judging us to be essentially bad in nature, and ready to condemn sinners to an eternity in hell, especially with Jesus as the example of how to be in the world. With this contradiction in his face from birth through young adulthood in an environment of emotional neglect and an absence of nurturing parents, Patrick was left by himself to contemplate his view of Self, the world, and God (influenced by the competing roles of religion and science).

In case you have never heard of Maslow's Hierarchy of Needs, it is a theory in psychology originally proposed by American psychologist Abraham Maslow in his 1943 paper, "A Theory of Human

Motivation" in the Journal Psychological Review. In his paper, Maslow provided a framework for understanding the human existence and development phases. According to Maslow's theory,

> (1) There are at least five sets of goals, which we may call basic needs. These are briefly physiological, safety, love, esteem, and self-actualization. In addition, we are motivated by the desire to achieve or maintain the various conditions upon which these basic satisfactions rest and by certain more intellectual desires. (2) These basic goals are related to each other, being arranged in a hierarchy of prepotency. This means that the most prepotent goal will monopolize consciousness...[18]

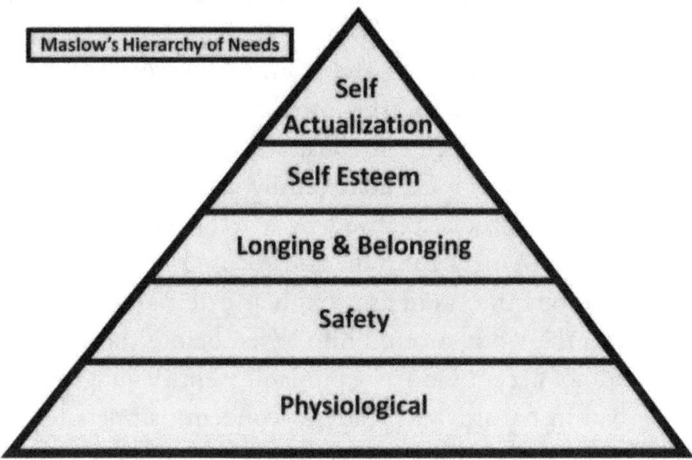

Maslow's theory originally proposed that the needs in the lower stages had to be fully satisfied before one could advance to the next stage, though Maslow later corrected this by recognizing that needs at each level of the hierarchy can be both partially satisfied and partially unsatisfied as the individual strives toward satisfying their basic needs and moving toward self-actualization.

One of the first things you might notice about the Integrated Self Model is that it resembles the pyramid traditionally used to represent Maslow's Hierarchy of Needs theory that we have come to know, even though it is said that Maslow himself never used a pyramid. Admittedly, the foundation of the Integrated Self Model is precisely a representation of the lower levels of Maslow's Hierarchy of Needs theoretical concept. Maslow's theory contributed not only to the foundation of the model based on the noted basic human needs, quality of life, personal identity, and significant relationships formed early on in life but also to the ego development process. We have overlapped Maslow's pyramid on top of the Integrated Self Model to demonstrate Maslow's major contribution and influence to this model as it relates to the ego development process.

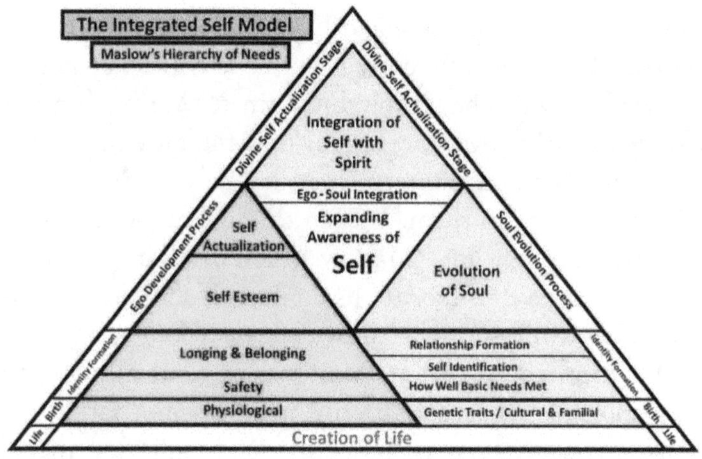

Based on personal experience and observation, Maslow's Hierarchy of Needs was missing more than supporting evidence. For Patrick, it only provided a reasonable way to understand the human experience in a one-dimensional way in terms of psychological cause-and-effect, the corresponding individualized view of the world, and the intrinsic influence that "human motivation" adeptly played.

The hierarchy of needs categorizes the "human motivation" into two groups,

> Maslow argued that all the needs can be grouped into two main classes of needs, which must be integrated for wholeness: deficiency and growth. Deficiency needs, which Maslow referred to as 'D-needs,' are motivated by a lack of satisfaction, whether it's the lack of food, safety, affection, belonging, or self-esteem... The greater the deficiency of these needs, the more we distort reality to fit our expectations and treat others in accordance with their usefulness in helping us satisfy our most deficient needs.[19]

"In any case, the psychological life of the person, in many of its aspects, is lived out differently when he is deficiency-need-gratification-bent and when he is growth-dominated...growth-motivated or self-actualizing."[20] "Maslow argues that the growth needs, such as self-actualization and transcendence, have a very different sort of wisdom associated with them."[21] Even through all of the challenges and struggles through life, "Maslow believed we are all capable of self-actualization, even if most of us do not self-actualize because we spend most of our lives motivated by deficiency.[22]

In his hierarchy of needs, Maslow was especially focused on the motivation of self-actualization. "So far as motivational status is concerned, healthy people have sufficiently gratified their basic needs for safety, belongingness, love, respect and self-esteem so that they are motivated primarily by trends to self-actualization."[23] "What self-actualization means is that a person is able to recognize they have potential and, as such, pursue after that highest potential. A self-actualized individual is someone who believes in becoming the very best that they can and pursues it to all ends."[24]

"The final piece of the [Hierarchy of Needs] is self-actualization. This is what happens after you have achieved significant mastery over the other four areas [of Maslow's Hierarchy of Needs]. This is where you are free enough to achieve incredible results and become a person who is fully alive, able to do great things without restriction."[25] "Self-actualizing people, those who have come to a high level of maturation, health, and self-fulfillment, have so much to teach us that sometimes they seem almost like a different breed of human beings."[26] The self-actualizer becomes "more truly himself, more perfectly actualizing his potentialities, closer to the core of his Being."[27]

> An important existential problem is posed by the fact that self-actualizing persons (and all people in their peak-experiences) occasionally live out-of-time and out-of-the-world (atemporal and aspatial) even though mostly they *must* live in the outer world... The healthy person is able to integrate both [inner and outer realities] into his life and therefore has to give up neither, being able to go back and forth voluntarily.[28]

While for the most part, our view of the ego development process aligns with Maslow's Hierarchy of Needs assessment, it is our belief that Maslow's theory only addresses the human experience in a large way but does not really address the influence of the spiritual experience and psychological impact that imbalance and incongruency between view of self, the world, the soul, and God have on the human experience and the human condition.

For us, Maslow's Hierarchy of Needs is represented in the Integrated Self Model as the identity formation stage and ego actualization stage, though elements may be found throughout the model when discussing motivation and self-actualization. This primary focus on the ego aspects of motivation and development by Maslow leaves much to be explained by the Integrated Self Model, which adds the spiritual aspects of the human experience in balance with the egoic experience addressed by Maslow. As such, this is in no way intended to refute or even minimize the significant contribution that Maslow's theory has provided to the world, and thus to the Integrated Self Model.

Section 3.8—Purpose of the Human-Spirit Experience

Each human being has both an ego and a soul to manage as integral parts of the human-spirit experience. Each of these parts brings its own agenda to the human-spirit relationship and each brings its own inherent strengths and weaknesses to this experience. The primary challenge to managing the interactions and conflicts between these parts is to find a way to balance the influence that each part has on the whole, and to create a thriving partnership that will encourage each part to consider and support the goals, purpose, and needs of the other.

The soul provides the echo of the spirit that creates the persistent sense that we are missing something, sometimes experienced as unexplainable angst or separation without remembering what from. The soul provides that longing to be someplace else or someplace better that can be explained as a pull back home without a conscious or subconscious knowing. The ego provides the drive, drama, story, and content for the perfectly imperfect human part of the human-spirit experience with the divine purpose of allowing Source to know itself, experientially.

> Our ego serves a purpose in our human evolution. For in the school of earth, we signed up to forget who we are, where we came from, and our connection to source. We must forget who we are in order to authentically choose our soul's path in our own free will. The path we choose is not judged as right or wrong. It just exposes more and more information about your own unique energetic field, soul blueprint, and personal evolution. It is merely our disruptor… our sense of reality innocently seen as truth, yet a mysteriously disguised illusion. We are on a mission to demask ourselves and unveil our own fundamental truths as we awake from our voluntary delusions. We set off the alarm clocks for

those vibrationally aligned to our frequency. As you elevate your truth, soul growth, you heal the collective, you contribute to the earth, you serve our universe. And for that I honor you. We can be disrupted and distracted, but never derailed from our mission of love. You cannot backslide soul growth. Every phase serves a purpose, a meaning and a purpose, if you choose to see it as such. Self-pity is a distraction. Guilt, shame, resentment is a disruption. Yet the polarization of these energies catapult you further into your evolution. The more pain, anguish, turmoil we experience, the deeper the satisfaction for love, forgiveness, peace, life. These low vibrations are not to be numbed or hidden. They are meant to be felt.[29]

Spirituality is about the journey. It is not about the destination. It is not about the abundance that's waiting for you at the end of the road. It is about the road. It is about the learning that occurs on that road. It is about experiencing the polarity of life… the good, the abundance, the love, the joy, the fulfillment, the happiness. But it is just as much so about experiencing the sadness, the grief, the despair, and all of those other "not so nice" feelings. Why? Because that is where soul growth happens. And also, you cannot appreciate one without experiencing the other. So spirituality is about the journey and the evolution that occurs while you are on that journey… Spirituality is so much more than being able to maybe see what potentially is coming in for you in the future. It is so much more than that. It is about evolution, soul growth…growing and learning and remembering who you are

> and where you come from. We are so much more than this physical 3D body. We are spirit first. But we are here in this physical body for evolution. Where does that evolution happen? It happens during the journey, the journey of life. So if you were focused on the destination, and that's all you're focused on, and you're hyper-fixated on that, you might want to take a step back.[30]

It is a critical, foundational assumption in the Integrated Self Model and related processes that problems and challenges in life are normal, even desired, for growth. A common theme throughout this book is that without hardship, struggle, and lessons, there is no growth. Without growth, there is no real movement during the human-spirit experience, and without movement, there is no way to work toward balance between the ego and soul. Without balance, there is no way to reach higher levels of consciousness, which leads us toward peace.

> Hardship is a fact of life. We will endure pain and misery in our lives, there is no getting around that. If you want to become more reliant on yourself, you must come to realize that pain and suffering are a guarantee and you must be prepared for it [at] all times. Not only that, but you must be willing to embrace hardship.[31]

PART 4

The Integrated Self Model

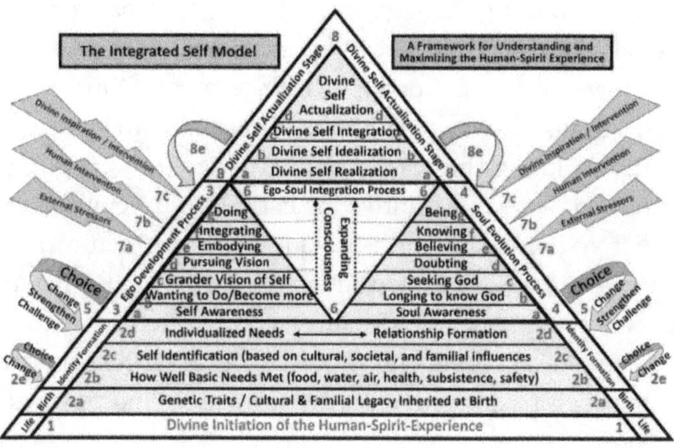

Section 4.1—Divine Initiation of Human-Spirit Experience

The Integrated Self Model starts with the beginning of human life, about which we all may have differing opinions regarding when we believe life begins. If we are to continue this discussion of the Integrated Self Model, we must put the need for agreement on those questions of why, when, and how life begins on hold. Life for each of us in this 3D world started somewhere, somehow and for some reason, so for the sake of this discussion, we will each have our own starting points regarding our existence in this human experience. The why and how is not central to the validity of the Integrated Self

Model, but a way to frame the picture and story of the human-spirit experience.

We, the authors, believe that it is the right of each individual to create our own belief system and personal story of how life began for us and why we are here. There are unlimited sources and opinions of the how and why and we have considered many perspectives of our origination and purpose while staying open to the differing opinions and belief systems of others. Even Patrick and Arianna don't fully agree on everything, which is one of the beautiful aspects of this human experience; that we all have the ability to think freely and find perspectives that feel supportive and empowering.

Since Patrick was little, Jesus served as his role model and spiritual guide for walking through life with love, compassion, kindness, and faith. Patrick was never really preoccupied with the unyielding pull to know the reason for his existence or humanity's existence. However, because it was part of the innate human nature to be in control and to know the reasons and answers to everything within our perception, it was imperative for Patrick to develop his own personal belief system that would provide him with comfort, support, hope, purpose, and even an ultimate destination. Rather innately, Patrick felt that he needed a roadmap from the Divine if he were to ever become lost along the way. His personal belief system and story were necessary for him to have a chance to find peace along the human-spirit journey.

In the pursuit of creating his story around the how and why of the human-spirit experience, Patrick gravitated toward the story offered in the book, *Conversations with God, Book 1* by Author Neale Donald Walsch. In chapter 1 of this book, God explained,

> Now in creating that which is "here" and that which is "there," God made it possible for God to know itself... My divine purpose of dividing Me was to create sufficient parts of Me so that I could know Myself experientially... My purpose in creating you, My spiritual offspring, was for Me to know Myself as God... My pur-

> pose for you is that you should know yourself as Me... [however] knowing something, and experiencing it, are two different things... Conceptual awareness was not enough for you... Once in the physical universe, you, My spirit children, could experience what you know as yourself...[32]

Another way to explain this concept from "Conversations with God" is that the Divine wanted to know itself, so it created the Divine Self. Knowing itself, that is, having knowledge of the existence of itself, is vastly different from experiencing itself, the Divine Self was split into an infinite number of pieces, which we will call Spirit. Spirit are pieces of the Divine Self, a part of the human-spirit experience as the human Soul (the light) in partnership with the human Ego (the dark), as the universe holds a duality of energy. Thus, the experiential nature of human existence was formed. Together, the soul and ego are a representation of Spirit (light and dark) as the human Self here in the 3D world. Spirit is a part of the Divine Self, the Divine. Therefore, it is our contention that we, each of us, are part of the whole of the Divine (Source).

In summary, it is our belief that the human-spirit condition and experience exist as ways for the Divine to experience parts of itself in real, more experiential ways. However, this model is not dependent on this underlying belief. The model is to be used according to each individual's unique beliefs, under the premise that we are spiritual beings having a human experience. The unconscious goal is to remember, rediscover, and reconnect with the Divine using the human experience as a catalyst to move toward this goal. At birth, we forget that we are connected to the Divine, and we perceive that we are alone and separated from our life source. We spend our lifetime unconsciously (at first), soulfully trying to remember who we are, where we came from, and to find our way back to the Divine.

Section 4.2—Basic Needs and Identity Formation Stage

During this identity formation stage, we develop a personal identity that is influenced by many factors. This identity is dynamic and constantly strengthening, weakening, or reforming depending on the choices we make and how congruent those choices are with our view of Self, our view of the world, and our view of the Divine.

(2a) Genetic Traits/Cultural and Familial Legacy Inherited at Birth

When we are born, we immediately inherit all of the cultural, societal, and familial experiences of our parents and their ancestors. The prevailing societal and familial norms when we are born immediately affect the formation of our view of ourselves and the world.

(2b) Basic Needs

Our view of ourselves is also directly affected by how well our basic needs are met. Basic needs are food, water, air, health, subsistence, nurturance, attachment, safety, certainty, and significance. This experience of having our basic needs met (or not) during our early years here on earth directly and dramatically affects our beliefs around our personal locus of control, that is, whether we have control over our experiences and future, or if the control is external to ourselves.

(2c) Self Identification

At a certain point in our human development, typically during the early teen years, we choose our personal identities (whether consciously or unconsciously) based on our life experiences and our inherited experiences and preferences. We choose who we are (or think we are) as individuals based on our individual view of ourselves and our view of the world, along with our view of Source. We continually define or redefine ourselves by the choices we make throughout our uniquely personal human lifetime.

(2d) Individualized Needs and Relationship Formation

Based on our identity of Self, we define our individualized needs and form relationships that support our identity. How well our individualized needs are met will determine whether our sense of Self is strengthened and supported or whether our Self is weakened or challenged, which will cause us to form or select a new identity.

(2e) Role of Choice in Creating Change during the Identity Formation Process

One of the main premises of the Integrated Self Model regarding life is, "Life is a series of choices. We define ourselves by the choices we make." Every moment we are making choices of how to be or not be in this world. Each and every choice we make serves to (a) move us further along the path we are currently on, (b) move us in a different direction, or (c) strengthen our current position and direction in life; thereby influencing our identity. We are constantly forming, reconsidering, and re-forming our own identity. With each choice that we make, either our identity gets stronger or we start questioning our identity. When we hit a specific threshold of change through our choices, our personal identity is altered. Changes in our personal identity are usually subtle and slow because every slight choice and change has an effect on the personal identity until that threshold required for change has been exceeded.

In the Integrated Self Model, each choice for identity change actually causes us to cycle back through the identity formation stage. The more integrated our self-identity, the more congruent our choices are (with the Self identity), the less dramatic the changes in identity will be, the less impact there is to our current lives, and consequently, the less struggle we experience. Our lives will then tend to be stable, uneventful, or even boring.

Typically, divine inspiration and/or divine intervention will challenge this stability because our purpose in life is to continue to have new experiences to foster growth, moving us to reconnect and reintegrate with the Divine. It is our belief that if we ignore divine inspiration, divine intervention will occur and reoccur until we make new choices or until we become complacent with our current station in life as we always have free will.

Section 4.3—Ego Development Process—Ego Actualization Stage

Once we have reached a certain level of integration of ego identity with our view of the world, we may enter the ego development process. In this stage, individuals become aware that they have unique egos and establish a sense of ego separate from other people and may move toward an idealistic version of themselves. We may stop or stall at any of the stages without progressing to the next stage.

(3a) Self Awareness (Ego Realization)

In this stage, we become aware that we have a unique ego and begin to establish a sense of ego separate from other people. It usually starts as a vague awareness at first until there is a clear understanding that we are unique individuals. We begin to consciously assess our current personal identity for potential and viability for engaging in real-life experiences in the physical 3D world.

(3b) Wanting to Do/Become More (Ego Individuation)

In this stage, we begin to differentiate ourselves from other individuals, choosing unique identities and ways of being in the world. Personal choices in this stage will strengthen, weaken, or challenge our Self-identity as it does in the identity formation stage. Our identity is never static and we are constantly cycling back through the identity formation stage and then back to the ego development stage with each choice we make.

(3c) Grander Vision of Self (Ego Idealization)

In this stage, we begin to create a grand vision and potential of our ego and our future Self. We begin to identify the steps necessary to achieve these grand visions of ego and form a blueprint or plan to experience this vision. However, this grand vision is limited by currently held beliefs and perceived limitations, and this vision will only be seen as *grand* relative to our current view of ourselves and the world. As we grow, we revisit our ultimate vision of ego and make new choices to support these even grander visions of ego.

(3d) Pursuing Vision of Self

As the grander vision of Ego takes shape through our planning, we begin to take the steps identified to achieve this vision. We begin to actively pursue this grander vision and somehow push through the doubt and fear that may linger from childhood issues and/or trauma. Step by step, little by little, we move closer to the vision of a better version of ego, of Self. If we are unable to move past doubts and fears from childhood, we may stall and remain stuck in this step.

(3e) Embodying (Vision of Self)

In this stage, we begin to realize a version of the grand vision of the ego. We start to embrace and embody who we want to be and attempt to act in accordance with our newly realized view of the ego. This is where you can say that practice makes perfect. This state of acting like the grand vision persists until either (1) this grand view of self becomes fully integrated as the identity of the Self, or (2) this grand view of self becomes changed or challenged through personal choice, divine intervention, or divine inspiration. Through these challenges, we may come to question our current identity, our imagined grand vision of Self. We may actually come to question (or lose) our strongly-held personal ego identity. When this happens, we will unconsciously loop back through the identity formation stage in order to figure out who we are and who we want to be and make new choices to support the modification of the current identity or the formation of an entirely new personal ego identity.

(3f) Integrating (Grand Vision of Self)

In this stage, we realize the grand vision of the ego. We embrace who we are and act in accordance with our view of the ego. As with the last stage, this condition holds true until changed or challenged through personal choices, divine intervention, or divine inspiration. Through these challenges, we may come to question our identity and our vision of Self and eventually lose our strongly held personal ego identity. We will then cycle back through the identity formation process to figure things out and make new choices supporting the formation of a new identity, solidifying and integrating into our vision of Self.

(3g) Doing (Ego Actualization)

Once we reach the goal of the ultimate grand vision of the ego and we are living our life with integrity; that is, we are doing things in our life that are congruent with the vision of the ego that has been reached and realized, we are then considered to be Ego actualized. Typically, ego actualization will require that the ego is in balance or in near balance with the soul. If both ego actualization and soul actualization are realized together, the Self is said to be self-actualized.

Section 4.4—Soul Evolution Process—Soul Actualization Stage

In the soul evolution process, we become aware that we have unique souls and that we have individual connections to Source; that is, we are a smaller version of the Divine. The focus on the soul is on connecting with Source through peaceful existence and being. The soul is not concerned with doing more (as the ego is) but rather being in a constant state of connection with Source. However, in the higher level of ego and soul integration, the soul will allow the ego to do more as long as the doing of the ego is in alignment with the being of the soul. Once we have reached a certain level of integration of soul identity with our view of the world, we may enter the soul actualization stage. We may stop or stall at any of the stages without progressing to the next stage.

(4a) Soul Awareness (Soul Realization)

In the soul awareness stage, we become aware that we have unique souls and begin to establish a sense of soul identity separate from other people. It starts as a vague awareness at first until there is a clear understanding that we are unique individual souls. This is commonly in today's age referred to as spiritual awakenings; however, we prefer the term soul remembering. There also becomes an awareness of the existence of the ego within the Self, with the understanding that the soul is separate from the ego.

(4b) Longing to know God

As the soul becomes aware, this awakening of the soul starts with a stirring, a sense of missing something. Once this happens, the stirring will continue to intensify, and a longing for that something missing will grow, and the evolution of the soul will persist.

(4c) Seeking God

The yearning will continue to grow and nag at the soul until there is a subconscious call-to-action to move toward an undeniable source and sense of being in peace. The soul will then begin actively seeking the Source of the yearning and take steps to find proof of an envisioned Source, even in the smallest way. The more that the soul looks for the Source, the more evidence of Source is discovered. However, the evidence is abstract in nature and any proof is intangible.

(4d) Doubting

As the intangible evidence of a Source mounts and the target of the search becomes more formed in the spiritual mind of the soul, the lack of actual, tangible proof that Source really exists causes the soul to start doubting the existence of Source. The doubting continues but the nagging and longing persists. Even while doubting, the Soul continues seeking Source, through with a reduced sense of urgency.

(4e) Believing

The evidence that was originally missed or doubted, along with the additional undeniable signs that Source does really exist eventually reaches a threshold and the doubting is turned into believing; that is, believing without a doubt that there is a Divine Source.

(4f) Knowing

Though it is not inevitable, if the seeking continues and the believing grows filling the Soul beyond belief, a certain threshold of knowing is reached and surpassed. The soul moves past all the need for evidence or proof, no longer doubting. There is only a knowing now that Source truly exists and is the Source of the Soul.

(4g) Being (Soul Actualization)

After coming to undoubtedly know the existence of God/Spirit as the Source, the Soul will relax into the knowing, into being connected to Source. In this state of being, we realize the grand vision of the Soul being connected to Source and becoming soul actualized. We embrace who we are and act in accordance with our view of the Soul. If both ego and soul actualization are realized together, the human Self is said to be self-actualized.

Section 4.5—Role of Choice in Identity Formation

The main premise of the Integrated Self Model regarding life and personal identity is: "Life is a series of choices. We define ourselves by the choices we make." Every moment we are making choices of how to be or how not to be in the world. Each choice for change actually causes us to cycle back through the identity formation process. Each choice serves to (a) move us further along the path we are currently on, (b) move us in a different direction, (c) strengthen our current position and direction in life, or (d) challenge our current position and direction.

The more integrated our self-identity is and the more congruent our choices are with our egoic self-identity, the less impact there is on our current lives and the less struggle we will have. Our lives will then tend to be stable, uneventful, and even boring. Typically, divine inspiration and/or divine intervention will challenge this stability because our purpose in life is to continue to have new experiences that foster growth, moving us to reconnect and reintegrate with the Divine. It is our belief that if we ignore divine inspiration, divine intervention will occur and reoccur until we make new choices or become complacent with our current station in life.

Section 4.6—Ego-Soul Integration Process

In the ego-soul integration stage, the focus of our attention in terms of the model is on the space between the ego development process and the soul evolution process, both literally and energetically. In this space between the ego and the soul is where the duality of consciousness and unconsciousness resides. There is a divinely architected correlation between the level of consciousness and the balance/imbalance of the ego and soul. As the imbalance between the ego and soul decreases and moves toward balance, the level of consciousness increases in the Self. When consciousness is at its lowest level, when there is significant separation or imbalance between the ego and the soul, the levels of angst and yearning are at their highest. Inversely, as consciousness increases, the levels of angst and yearning decrease in the Self, and there is incremental movement toward balance and peace.

For the ego-soul integration process, balance is not the only critical factor required for the full integration of Self. Congruency is the other critical factor (along with balance) required for the realization of the fully integrated Self. As the ego and soul come into balance, the level of self-integration is dependent on how congruent the Self is between its belief systems and how it operates in the physical world and spiritual world.

The level of self-integration is dependent on the level to which the following questions can be affirmed: Are you living congruently with your view of the world? Is your view of the world congruent with your view of God or Spirit? Are you living a balanced life, a life of mind and spirit, a life of contentment and peace?

(6a) Expanding Consciousness

As our consciousness or awareness of the *true* nature of this world and our *true* connection to the Divine grows, the connection between the ego and soul increases. At the lower levels of consciousness, the ego and soul are seen as the same with little or no individuation of the pieces. At the lower levels of consciousness, we may not even have a sense that we have a soul, or that there is something bigger than ourselves.

As our consciousness or awareness of the *true* nature of the world and our connection to the Divine grows, the connection of the ego and soul increases and the level of consciousness expands (and increases). As consciousness expands, we sense that we have an ego and a soul that we perceive as separate, unconnected parts of the whole, which causes internal confusion and conflict. At the upper levels of consciousness, we understand that the ego and soul are both separate and connected, but together they are the whole of the human Self.

The Integrated Self Model addresses the influence that the individualized view-of-God and any incongruence/imbalance between the individualized view of Self and view of God might play in the internal confusion, stress, and anxiety for each person as they move toward Divine Self Actualization (or Transcendence, as labeled in Maslow's Hierarchy of Needs). This imbalance/incongruency in the Integrated Self Model is assumed to be and is referred to in the model as the Level of Consciousness, as personally experienced by each individual.

When we discuss the levels of consciousness and expanding awareness that use relative terms to explain the differences, we do not intend to promote the idea that one level of consciousness is more desirable than another. With each level of consciousness, you get a different experience, both human and spiritual. We understand that it is both human nature and the nature of relative concepts to invoke comparison. Instead of looking at the levels of consciousness as a hierarchy, we find it best to only consider them for yourself, as an individual to understand where you are on the scale and what you may need to work on in terms of healing and growth in order to increase your own personal level of consciousness and improve your quality of life through balanced growth. There is so much value in the lower levels of consciousness. It is where we meet our wounds, unhealed parts of ourselves, and illuminate the shadows that have not been integrated yet.

(6b) Balance / Imbalance

As we discussed previously, the Integrated Self Model is about balancing the ego (mind) development and the soul evolution. If you concentrate on one aspect of Self while neglecting the other, you will experience an imbalance in your human Self, and this imbalance may create conflict, confusion, frustration, or misalignment, thereby creating incongruency and causing you to find ways to balance or go through the ego development or soul evolution processes again until congruency is realized.

Section 4.7—Role of Stressors, Intervention, and Inspiration

The physical 3D world is a constant source of pressure, challenges, and hardships in the form of external stressors, human intervention, divine intervention, and divine inspiration. They provide the opportunities for choice, change, and growth.

(7a) External Stressors

The 3D world is a constant source of challenges, difficult situations, and hardships in the form of external stressors. These external stressors are the physical, nonhuman influences on our day-to-day lives. These external stressors can include weather, nature, physics, gravity, the sun, the moon, and other physical elements in this 3D world. While out of scope for this current version of the model, many people are also influenced externally by the quantum physical and metaphysical worlds. In any case, any real 3D physical world influencers that exist outside of the physical/spiritual Self can be considered external stressors.

(7b) Human Intervention

During our lives, we come into near-constant contact with other self-focused humans trying to navigate the physical world the best they can. These ego-driven people provide continuous challenges and opportunities that influence our lives in the form of human interventions. While these other-human interactions are always self-serving from their own personal perspectives, these same challenges and opportunities, from our own unique perspective, can be considered positive, negative, or neutral in the present moment and then ultimately turn out to be positive, negative, or neutral at some point in the future. There is nothing ever certain about human interactions except for in the present moment, and even then, the certainty is only based on our personal perspective in the moment.

(7c) Divine Inspiration/Divine Intervention

Throughout our lives, the Divine presents endless opportunities for making choices that will influence the direction that our path in life takes. These opportunities can and will be presented in many forms as seemingly positive or negative events. In the model, these opportunities from the Divine are grouped into two categories: Divine intervention and Divine inspiration.

Divine intervention is when Source provides opportunities for change or growth that are presented as real-life events, both positive and negative, that encourage or force people to reassess their lives, confront their existence, and face inevitable, unavoidable change, usually through personal challenges, setbacks, adversity, struggle, and tragedy. Divine intervention is an actual experience in the 3D world that is of divine orchestration that causes (or forces) us to respond in a certain way and to move, perhaps unwittingly, in a direction that will provide the opportunity for choice and change.

Divine inspiration is when we are divinely impressed with a thought, vision, or perceived experience that inspires us to act or change our life's direction, whether it takes hold immediately or eventually through a planted seed that grows over time. The Divine provides inspiration through mostly unconscious impressions, not rooted in the physical world, though these Divine inspirations or impressions may come from events and experiences in the physical world. Much of the time, Divine inspiration is confused with ego self-talk, and it takes much time to practice and learn to discern between Divine inspiration and ego self-talk.

Section 4.8—Divine Self-Actualization Stage

In this stage, we become aware that even though we have unique human souls and we have individual connections to God, we are all connected with each other and with Source. We become aware that we come from Source, that we are each a part of the Divine, that we have a Divine Soul, and that we are each the Divine Self. Our focus is turned from the physical 3D world to the soulful vision of the Divine

Self being back with Source by an ascension through the levels of consciousness toward the uppermost levels of enlightenment. Once we have reached full integration of the Divine Self with the Divine, we return to Source again at the end of this lifetime.

At this point in the model, we would like to issue a disclaimer related to the divine self-actualization stage. The work on expanding consciousness and moving toward enlightenment must be an intentional and conscious process. As the integrated Self moves closer and closer to Source, the fully integrated Self will separate more and more from the physical 3D world. The integrated Self will no longer feel a part of the physical world and will most likely enter what the spiritual community refers to as "hermit mode" during this transition process. "Hermit mode" is when we isolate ourselves to a degree from engaging and participating in life with other people or draw back our energy to go internally. It is very important at this stage to ground your energy and connect to nature as we begin to re-engage with the world and continue the human-spirit experience.

In relative terms, few people will relate to this part of the model, and even fewer will actually complete the ascension back to the Divine during a lifetime. Most people who enter this stage at some point in the process will, (1) remember their unique purposes in this lifetime, (2) reengage with the physical 3D world to continue their respective missions, and (3) consciously delay their rejoining with the Divine until later in their lives or the eventual end of their lifetime in this world.

(8a) Divine Self Realization

Once our consciousness advances to the upper levels, we will come to realize that we are all connected with the Divine. Our connection to the Divine increases, introducing the potential of moving further into the Divine integration stage. However, we may stay in this stage without advancing any further. When we realize that we are connected to and part of the Divine, it is difficult to forget this, even through the choices we make. Being able to connect with so many people through social media we have seen countless times that many agree and their personal experience matches with this idea that we cannot unknow what we now know. With Divine realization comes the ability to experience bliss, though this may not happen if we do not choose to see through the perspective of abundance and experience the present moment.

(8b) Divine Self Idealization

Divine self idealization is the next stage where we develop an ideal image of the Divine. We begin to create an ultimate, grand vision of ourselves as part of the Divine by beginning to identify steps necessary to maintain and strengthen this grand vision of an intimate relationship with Source; however, this grand vision is limited by our held beliefs that our ego and soul are separate and that our ego self must be shed in order to achieve Divine integration.

(8c) Divine Self Integration

In divine self integration, we understand that we must fully integrate the ego and soul together while maintaining the individuality of pieces as each part is of the whole. We fully understand that the ego and soul are part of our Divine Self, which is an intimate part of the Divine. We successfully find balance and harmony between the ego and soul, becoming fully integrated and creating our Divine Self Identity.

(8d) Divine Self Actualization / One with God

In this final stage of the model, we realize the grand vision of our Divine Self and are considered to be Divine Self-Actualized. This is where our fully integrated Divine Self (Ego-Soul) becomes fully integrated with the Divine while maintaining our own Divine Self (Ego-Soul) identity. We fully understand now that we are both the Divine and part of the Divine. We are once again one with Source.

(8e) Decision to Proceed or Reengage

As previously mentioned, the work on expanding consciousness and moving toward enlightenment must be conscious and intentional. As the Integrated Self moves through Divine Self Integration, the fully integrated Self may find itself spiritually separating more and more from the physical world. The main premise of this model and publication is to bring about a new lens of looking at mental health, so it would not be within our integrity if we did not advise you to seek help if you find yourself detaching from the human experience. Within the scope of this model, it is a normal phenomenon to experience at this stage. However, the significance of having a support system, grounding yourself, and prioritizing your health and wellness is of the utmost importance.

PART 5

Taking Steps Toward Balance and Growth (by Patrick)

Section 5.1—The Steps Toward Balance and Growth

The Integrated Self Model is a representation of my life encompassing the real-world challenges, lessons, and inevitable personal growth that I have experienced, including core childhood issues, the focus on personal growth over spiritual growth, the internal conflict caused by the imbalance of the ego and soul, and then the conscious and deliberate steps taken to create balance; thereby, expanding consciousness as I was drawn toward God, the Divine.

The first step to understanding how to use the Integrated Self Model personally and effectively is to understand where you currently land on the model regarding (1) how well your basic needs were met as a child, (2) the state of your early and current significant relationships, (3) your personal identity and personality, (4) the current state of your mental health, and (5) your current view of God and of the world. Once you understand approximately where you are, you will then be able to create a self-development plan in order to focus your growth work, either by yourself or with the support of a mental health practitioner, coach, mentor, or therapist.

One of the best ways to gain this understanding is to document your personal story as you remember it today. Actually, we are going to write our story and then rewrite it. The purpose of this is to understand who we are today, all of it. We have lived a lifetime with this story, with this identity that, if it was not consciously and deliberately considered, chosen, and built, it was subconsciously installed. It was unconscious-subconscious programming for who you are. This story that you are writing is a story about your mental and spiritual health. Who are you? Who are you really? I am going to walk you through the process of first writing your story from your perspective, assessing the story, and then rewriting your story from a conscious and balanced perspective.

When you come to write your story, which is an exercise to better know yourself, Author Michael Singer tells us,

> It starts to become a serious question: "Who am I? Who is having all these physical, emotional, and mental experiences." So you contemplate this question a little deeper. This is done by letting go of the experiences and noticing who is left. You will begin to notice who is experiencing the experience. Eventually, you will get to a point within yourself where you realize that you, the experiencer, have a certain quality. And that quality is awareness, consciousness, an intuitive sense of existence.[33]

The very first question that must be answered before we get into anything else is: What is our story? What do we tell ourselves about the way our life went, the way our childhood, teenage, young adulthood, or even mid-life or senior years went? What do we tell ourselves and what do we tell others? Much of the time we fabricate what we are telling other people about ourselves or how life is going. We create this facade or persona to present an image of a person that we want them to think of us as, or who we want the world to see us as.

Our inner confusion, inner conflict, and inner stress or even depression are caused by the difference between who we present to the world and others, and who we believe we are on the inside, in our subconscious. Fortunately, if you do choose to do personal growth work, you can close the gap quite a bit, but typically we still present a persona to the world that may not be 100 percent who we are inside. Who are you really? Who would you like to be? We are now going to write the story and consider who we really are. We will document that story and do some honest self-reflection and consideration of who we really are, and who we really want to be.

Not only do we get a chance now to consciously consider how we want to understand and rewrite the story of our past, but we can also now seize the opportunity to alter the trajectory of our future Self. We can develop a fresh perspective and write the story that is yet to be through a life lived well and consciously. Transformational Mindset Coach Tiffany Gingrich emphasizes this point,

> If we have never stopped and identified and examined our belief systems, then often we're just living on default; just whatever we were taught when we were young. As adults we're walking around thinking those same thoughts all day long… and if we identify and we go in and examine, then we're not living by default; we're actually choosing and we're creating conscious awareness. Awareness is almost enough to make the changes. Awareness is such a big part of the process of personal growth that, when you become aware that you're doing that thing that you don't want to be doing, that's where the power is. It's in the stopping and being consciously aware… You can create conscious awareness around patterns in your life; around your habits; your behaviors; the emotions that you feel every day. And it all begins with awareness. Awareness around what the identity that you've had about yourself is, who you think you are in this world… Remember, your beliefs are shaping your entire reality. The stories that you are telling yourself are dictating how you live your entire life… and

> the people that you surround yourself with are dictating what you believe is even possible for you. The good news is you have complete control over your beliefs, your stories, and who is in your inner circle.[34]

For this exercise of explaining and demonstrating the process of writing our story, I will walk you through my own personal story and my personal perspective because it is very important to stress that we all go through things throughout the human-spirit experience; the hard times, the happy times, challenges, success, struggles and victories, so maybe you will relate to parts of my story. We are all spiritual beings having a human experience that is unique to each and every one of us.

Everyone comes out of their childhood with an issue (at least one, for sure) and I know it was more than one issue for both myself and Arianna. The idea is that this is just what it is to be human, to be presented with challenges and situations that are going to cause us to experience human emotion, feeling, and thought. A real human being who is presented with problems and challenges is also offered options and opportunities to grow through pain, loss, and grief to grow through life. Everyone is imperfectly perfect and neither Arianna nor I have met anyone that has said, "Yeah! I had a perfect childhood!" Even children from the same family that have shared life events will each have different experiences which creates a different thought process and feeling about those events.

Take note that while you go through this process of writing your story and identifying who you really are, you will need to become the observer of your mind (both the conscious and subconscious minds) and how they interact with each other. As Michael Singer says,

> By watching the mind, you will notice that it is engaged in the process of trying to make everything okay. Consciously remember that this is not what you want to do, and then gently disengage. Do not fight it. Do not fight your mind.

> You will never win. It will either beat you now, or you will suppress it and it will come back and beat you later. Instead of fighting your mind, just don't participate in it.[35]

Section 5.2—Understand and Document Your Personal Story

To accomplish this story-writing exercise, I will break my story down into pieces. The first time period to look at your story is the foundational years, the ages from zero to seven, which are primarily when your brain is the most malleable. This is where you are the most impressionable and programmable due to the state of your brain waves which are in theta. Theta state, which is the state of hypnosis, is when you are the most susceptible to subconscious programming. During these years, you are being programmed by your experiences, how you perceive those experiences, and how your body reacts to those experiences.

In essence, it is a strong mixture of both positive and negative programming. The not-so-good fact is that we tend to focus on our negative experiences, especially during these early years of life. As we continue to progress, we tend to lean into those negative programming experiences because the primary job of our ego (subconscious mind) is to watch for danger and keep us safe. Due to this focus on negative experiences and the role of the ego, we give very little weight to our positive experiences and achievements.

Early Childhood Years (Age zero to seven years old)

I was born into a New York Italian family in the 1950s as the first-born son, the third of four children, with two older sisters and a younger brother. Even though I was third in the birth order, being born the first son in an Italian American family, represents such a mixed bag right away. Immediately, there was the prestige of being the first-born son in our family, which meant that my two (older) sisters probably felt pushed aside. Just imagine the attention that the first-born son gets in an ethnic family after waiting six years for a son.

From the age of birth to five years old specifically, I have very little memory of that time. I think that I may only have some memories related to some photos that I had seen and from stories that I might have been told. There was no physical or sexual abuse present in the core family at all. My one and only spanking in my life was when I was about six years old. The spanking occurred because I would not eat my vegetables and I cried to get some attention and sympathy. My father literally said, "I'll give you something to cry about," and he spanked me. This quickly taught me that feelings were not allowed, and there are consequences to expressing myself. That was the first time and the last that I got spanked. There were some incidents with my oldest sister as a teenager being mouthy to my father. It was not pleasant, but it definitely was a lesson for us younger children growing up behind her. It was clear that our thoughts and opinions were not appreciated or valued. I am telling you this because it is a significant part of my story. Our stories are rich in detail and evidence that can point to why we are the way we are.

My memory is that I was very close to my youngest sister who was a year and a half older than myself, and I remember feeling that she was my best friend. When she started school and wasn't home all of the time, I felt that I lost my best friend. There was obviously no bad intention but as a five-year-old child, I had felt that my friend all my life had left me. My first day of school was a bit traumatic inside a large elementary school. I became confused as to where my classroom was located and I started to cry. My first day out in the real world on my own provided enough evidence to me that the world outside of my home was confusing, scary, and maybe even unsafe. Life went on, but my indelible memory from birth to seven years old held the story that I was basically alone.

There was not a lot of personal interaction in my family. My siblings and I learned to stay away from each other to avoid any kind of interaction that may cause arguments, noise, or stress to prevent getting in trouble. Feelings were not really allowed in the family unless it came from the adults (primarily my father or the other men) and it was mainly to communicate annoyance, disapproval, and anger. Even with this displayed behavior by my father, my mother was (to me) the head of the household, seemingly in control of everyone's behavior in our family system.

As a child, a woman being in charge of the household all seemed natural and normal because my grandmother was the head of the Diorio family. My grandfather (my father's father) died when my father was thirteen years old, and my grandmother became the de facto patriarch of the family (not the matriarch as you might expect). My grandmother was of German descent and more of a stoic, serious person and I adored her. My grandmother and my aunt (father's sister) were the ones who nurtured me and I believe they nurtured all of us as children. I believe that my father and mother were both Myers-Briggs personality type ISTJ (Introversion-Sensing-Thinking-Judging)[36] and that most of their interactions and processing were through thinking and judging; that means schedules, promptness, rules, plans, and doing things only one way (their way), and that is all.

There was no coloring outside the lines allowed, figuratively and literally. Essentially, what I experienced was emotional neglect, which is what I believe happens when we as children do not get our emotional needs fulfilled. We did not get attended to by our parents in an emotional way to allow us to feel, process, and understand our feelings.

For me now, this story does not invoke sorrowful feelings of not being loved or not being loved enough. For me now, this is just background information at this moment that completes my story, and we will use this information later in this exercise. My belief system says to me that, when I was born, I was also the same personality type as my parents (or at least predisposed to it). Therefore, I seem to naturally fit into a rule-based household and society. I believe that being predisposed to this similar personality type from birth allowed me to come out of childhood in a better situation, less damaged, and less traumatized than my siblings.

I was also told by my mother later in life that my father would tell my siblings, "Why can't you be more like Pat? Why can't you do things more like your brother?" I am really sorry to hear that; however, I never heard that for myself. My father never directly praised or complimented me for anything. There was no validation for me, or any of us during our childhood. There was very little conversation between my father and me, and that made for deep father-validation issues.

We are still talking here about my experience being in the ages from birth to five years old. The feeling I remember the most was that I felt alone, invisible. I also remember rather vividly being told as a small child while riding in the backseat of our car with my brother and sister that, "Children should be seen and not heard," and when trying to join the adult conversation taking place in the front seat my mother said, "Little pitchers have big ears." It was clear that our thoughts and opinions as children were not wanted, which my young brain translated to mean that I was not valued, personally.

From age five years old and on, I started becoming more conscious and aware of life and significant life events. I remember that the television was becoming a big deal in the news, being relatively new at the time. In the 1950s and at the age of five years old, I remember that the color television was in its early stages and that we still had a black and white television in our home. Being left to take care of myself, television quickly became my best friend. I learned about proper family behaviors from television shows like, *Leave It to Beaver* and *Father Knows Best* as well as how to take care of others and be the unseen hero behind the scenes from *The Lone Ranger* among many others. Yes, I am a boomer.

As you relive your life, this exercise of documenting your story may get to be long, and hopefully not too stressful or traumatizing for you. However, I urge you to not rush through your story and to literally write it down to document it. A lot of my personal history that I am sharing with you right now, I probably would not have thought about in any real detail, at least not consciously if I hadn't done this exercise for myself. There is a difference between knowing something in your subconscious (that is, unconsciously) and bringing these stored memories and guarded emotions into the conscious mind. When you take your time and provide attention and energy to your feelings while talking about these experiences (i.e., telling your story), it gives air to these experiences; it provides them light.

At first, exploring these experiences might even give power to these memories while shining your light on them. However, after a while the emotional energy drains and it just becomes our story, just part of who we are, our history, and maybe even some of the things that we have grown past are seen in a new light so we can now be proud of ourselves for being able to circumvent the programming, or even reprogram ourselves in the best of cases.

In the worst of cases, we may still be haunted or traumatized by these memories and sometimes, it is just a feeling that gets stored inside your body, inside the crevices of your mind, and deep into the subconscious. It is there, and it will remain there until you are able to deal with it and find a place where you can put it on a shelf, put it in the back seat of the car, and let you drive through life as the now adult Self, taking special care of your inner child.

Later Childhood Years (Age seven to twelve years old)

The next phase of life that I will cover is approximately from the ages of seven to twelve years old. This time period is around when we are typically in elementary school, the time just after our early childhood experiences and just before we really begin to develop a personal identity during the teen years that we will take into the real world as young adults. During our years from ages seven to twelve, we are living life through the lens of our childhood experiences, mostly finding supportive evidence for our strengths and our issues, thereby allowing these personal characteristics to set in and become even more solidified in the subconscious mind. Unless you are in an abusive situation, our lives tend to continue on from the early childhood years through this period of human growth, just carrying your experiences with you from those early times.

Developmentally, our young minds are evolving from thinking in concrete, black-and-white terms to more abstract, colorful ways of seeing life and the world. During this time, we are experiencing life differently than our childhood years. We are not quite as small and not quite as vulnerable, and we increase our vocabulary and ability to understand and communicate in ways that we could not when we were younger. We are now entering and becoming part of the real world in real ways through attending school and participating in community social events. Undesirable family behaviors now risk public exposure if they are continued or escalated. Society mostly supports and even promotes a "don't ask, don't tell" policy when it comes to discussing the mental health struggles of families. I will continue on with my personal story during these years of my life experience.

Besides the lack of emotional nurturing and validation from my parents during my early childhood years, there was no abuse or trauma evident to me, then or now; so I must conclude that there was none. Even emotional neglect was not brought into my conscious mind during this time, though the lack of nurturing and validation remained stored in my subconscious mind. Maybe this was because I was able to get the needed attention and validation from school experiences. I excelled scholastically in school, receiving ample attention and validation from my teachers and grades. Even though I did not get actual validation at home, I did not get negative attention at home either. As long as I brought home good grades, I was left alone. My siblings may not have fared as well. This time period for me and the family was fairly quiet. There was not much drama and there was no trauma as far as I recall. I continued to stay by myself, out of sight, out of mind, and out of trouble.

Even now as we are getting older and we were able to communicate better, the lack of direct personal communication and intentional validation from my parents persisted. The language of love from my parents was definitely not words of affirmation, physical touch, or quality time. I have concluded that the primary language of love for my parents was acts of service. For my father, this took the form of working hard for ten to twelve hours a day, six to seven days a week.

For all intents and purposes, there was little to no communication between myself and my father. For my mother, acts of service took the form of being a stay-at-home mother, providing a clean and orderly home, and tending to our basic needs related to day-to-day life and school. My mother would only leave our small home weekly for groceries, church, and the family visit to my aunt's house. When at home, my mother would mainly sit at our kitchen table working on crossword puzzles and there was very little interaction with us. My mother's solitary, hermit-like behavior implicitly created and reinforced the feeling that people and the world are unsafe and that it was best to stay by ourselves even when living in a small house as a family of six.

As for elementary school, I attended a small Catholic school for grades first through eighth primarily with religious nuns as teachers. For the most part, the nuns were wonderful and my time in this elementary school was positive and supportive. Everything was going great until toward the end of my sixth-grade year when, traditionally each year, the sixth-grade boys would play the seventh-grade boys in a softball game. There were not many boys in my class so when it came time for the game, ten out of the thirteen boys would get picked to participate, and I was not chosen to play. I was small in size, and I hadn't really played sports with my father or siblings before so I was left out of the game. You'd think this would be such a sad moment for me, and it was disappointing, but it turned out to be the most significant event and major turning point in my life.

On that fateful day, something clicked inside of me bringing me to life. In that summer between sixth and seventh grade, I was determined to teach myself how to play baseball. My obsessive-compulsive tendency became laser-focused on my goal. At my house, my father had added a room with a brick wall on the outside. During the summer break from school, I bought a superball (a compressed rubber ball) and began to throw the ball against the brick wall, slowly at first. I began throwing harder and harder until I had developed extremely quick reflexes like no other. From that point on, I would make sure I was always athletic so I would not risk being left out.

For the rest of my life, I was always above average in sports and really everything because I could not see myself as less than average ever again. My own voice told me in my head that I would need to learn how to extravert myself more or I would end up being lost in the world. I now needed to take control of myself and my own life and start acting consciously. I didn't know exactly what I needed to do but I was clear about the persona of a brave, confident boy that I needed to adopt and present to the world. There was no doubt, no fear, just determination. The memory of that fateful day of how it felt not being picked or included was the driving force for the rest of things to come.

From the start of seventh grade, I kept excelling and continued attracting positive attention. I was picked by my teacher to be the president of the seventh-grade boys club, I entered a speech contest and then in eighth grade, I was voted president of the class and captain of the school's safety patrol. I became the observer of this person, whom I did not recognize, but quickly came to respect and trust. I am telling you this story about myself because I want you to understand that you have stories just like this about you, in you. You have your own stories that you can point to, moments of choice, moments that lifted you up, or choices that kept you down. You have to look at these situations as learning moments, take note of them as just being information, and then move forward.

For me, this period of seven to twelve years old started out as rather uneventful and ended with a positive, life-changing turn of events that started a new way of being in the real world. This turn of events set me up nicely for the identity creation and selection process in the next stage of growth, which I have found to be a typical age for solidification or modification in our personal identity formation. Even though this time of positive outside attention and growth, the evidence and effects of not being able to gain my parents expressed validation, sense of belonging, caring, and love continued to build, opaquely hidden by the new persona of self-empowerment and self-esteem.

Teenage years (Ages twelve to eighteen years old)

Twelve years old seems to be a typical age that I've seen with myself, my family, and clients where seemingly sudden changes occur in personality, identity, and deciding who to be in the world. The construction of a new identity does not happen to everyone; many of us will continue with the default identity that we developed organically from birth to age twelve. This default identity is sometimes strong, healthy, and thriving, and sometimes hurt, unhealthy, and fearful. If we consciously perceive that our existing personal identity will not support us properly and safely in the adult world, we will typically choose a personal identity that we believe will better protect and support us as adults. Around age twelve, we either continue on into the teenage stage with our current identity, whether chosen unconsciously or consciously, or we instinctively construct a new persona and identity that we will try out during these teenage years, checking to see if it fits, and making adjustments as we discover what works well and what does not.

For me, this period of life was very stable and confirmed the persona that I constructed around age twelve. I started in the ninth grade of a private Catholic high school with positive energy and high self-confidence which I had perfected during seventh and eighth grade. My high school experiences were the proving grounds for my constructed persona with very good outcomes, with maybe one exception.

Being in several leadership positions in elementary school led to my desire to continue being in positions of leadership and influence, so I ran for one of the elected student council positions in ninth grade. It quickly became apparent that my coming to this private high school from a very small elementary school created a disadvantage for me when it was time for voting on the candidates. Those candidates for student council who came from larger school districts were known by a larger portion of the freshman class, which resulted in their election. This experience of losing was very humbling to me—the self-proclaimed big man on campus for the eighth-grade class of only thirty-six students. Reality settled in about the possibility of never being in a leadership position in school again, so I comfortably settled back into being introverted and invisible among a high school student body of about two thousand.

As an extension of my newly formed athletic identity through practicing my skills and confidence, I joined the freshman football team. There were no tryouts so everyone who reported to the first practice made the team; however, I was initially overlooked because of my relatively smaller size. Not deterred, I quickly drew positive attention and earned a starting position where I was later named defensive captain for the last game of the freshman football season. My junior varsity football experience was more balanced since we mixed with the upperclassmen who had more experience, which provided me with more chances to make mistakes and grow.

Overall, high school football was an extremely positive experience for me. It helped to build confidence in my athletic abilities among my peers. However, after two years of high school football, I decided not to continue playing. I was very disappointed, and maybe even depressed, that none of my family had attended a single football game. Misguidedly, I stopped playing in order to spite myself as a consequence of not being worthy of my parents' validation and love.

Scholastically speaking, I was considered to be in the second-highest scholastic group of freshman students, allowing me to perform well in high school with intellectually equal peers. This made for just the right amount of challenge and growth to keep things interesting for me. My parents continually paid little attention to me and my grades because I had consistently been a well-performing student since elementary school, especially compared to my three siblings. As a result, I settled into being an excellent student because it came effortlessly to me and also assured me that I would be invisible (or at least transparent) within my high school environment, while simultaneously feeling invisible within my family system at home.

Adult years (Ages eighteen years and older)

By the time we are out of high school, we have developed and tried out the personal identity that we will take into young adulthood and carry our wounds behind our adult facade. We may learn how to hide all our trauma, abuse, invalidation, rejection, hurt, challenges, and failures that we have experienced up until this point. By this time, we have mostly decided who we are going to be in the world, that is, until something happens to challenge our view of Self and our personal identity, or until we experience some form of divine inspiration, divine intervention, or even human intervention.

For me and most people, human interventions are the most challenging because they are usually right in your face, on the other side of someone else's ego, or on the other side of someone else's growth experience. It is usually not pleasant at all and we do our best to stay out of the way of people having ego reactions to their programming as a kid, or perhaps reactions to their stored memories of abuse, neglect, or trauma that they have experienced. Of course, while we are trying to avoid the human tendencies of others to act in their best interest, we struggle to stay out of our own way as we also act in our own self-centered, self-serving humanness, and we have our own ego reactions in response to others.

I have a heart for people, especially for those who have not started to heal from their early childhood trauma or subconscious programming. It is a hard position to be in but is something we all have to work with. As difficult and painful as it is to confront our childhood demons, this is precisely what we have to do; we have to do the work. We have to meet ourselves exactly where we are at the moment and create a safe and supportive environment to heal. We have to begin to ask ourselves important and uncomfortable questions: What are those childhood experiences that shaped who we are currently? What factors caused our personal identity to be developed or constructed in this specific way? As we enter adulthood, our personal identity is synonymous with the ego until we start folding in the spiritual component that comes with the awakening of the soul, usually later in life.

For my personal story in young adulthood, I instinctively knew that I could no longer operate as the invisible, academic student through life if I was going to find a place in the world where I would be productive, safe, and seen. I could no longer be pouting about how my parents and family did not care about me, my football games, my grades, or my existence for that matter. While I took control of myself in the real adult world, it was apparent that I was leaning into my childhood experiences of having to take care of myself; however, it was also obvious that subconsciously I was dragging around my negative childhood experiences on my shoulders. My personal identity was certainly a mixture of all my childhood experiences, as you would expect as an objective observer. Of course, at that time, my conscious mind was not directly aware of the influences of my subconscious, egoic mind.

My first thought while writing this part of my story was to say that from the age of twenty, my life was rather uneventful and stable. I now understand through this conscious inspection of that period of my life that I was moving through life as that persona and identity that I had constructed. But just under the surface of my conscious mind lurked my subconscious mind with all of that reactive programming from my childhood.

Prior to gaining an awareness of my subconscious programming and how this negatively impacted my life, relationships, and self-image, I was living in a daze, sleepwalking under the influence of my childhood programming. Later in this book, we will specifically identify and discuss these childhood issues that controlled my actions and reactions and kept me safe. For the purpose of this story-writing exercise, I will now outline the observable behaviors and symptoms of this subconscious programming.

As is typical for most people with childhood issues around their parents, my adult relationships resembled my relationship with my mother. Even though I spent much time telling the story of my father's validation issues, my mother was emotionally unavailable to me and my siblings. She operated in the world as a logical thinker, not a feeler. While my mother did attend to our basic needs, there was little affection and an absence of nurturing provided. This does not make my mother a bad person or a poor mother as she was not predisposed to feelings, affection, and nurturing even when it was with her own children. This caused me to look for emotionally unavailable women who were not outwardly affectionate. I have come to understand that I had developed an anxious-attachment style and was attracted to women who had an avoidant-attachment style. I was searching for relationships and romantic partners who were not able to love me the way I needed, which repeated the same feelings from my early childhood relationships with my mother (and my father).

The personal identity that I had constructed when I was twelve years old as a confident, extraverted, high-performing leader was very supportive of my desire to be seen as above average and viewed in a positive light. From that moment of decision to assert myself in the real world, I consistently over-achieved and embodied the "mind over matter" and "fake it till you make it" mantras that drove everything I did or planned to do.

Right out of high school, I secured a job as a night crew stock clerk in a grocery store and quickly moved up to night crew manager, dairy clerk, dairy manager, and so on until I was the grocery department manager. Even with this apparent success, this did not fulfill me. I was programmed from an early age that I always needed to do more if I were to gain/earn approval and validation from my father. My mother would tell me that my father bragged about me to others, but I never received any praise directly. This experience coupled with the fact that my father would not teach me his trade as an excavating contractor felt to me like rejection and invalidation; all the while my mother would tell me that my father wanted better for me than the hard life he was living and working. I still perceived this as rejection.

You can see how my advancement through the ranks in the grocery store to manager would not be enough for me and the subconscious motivation for my father's validation persisted. Predictably, I went back to college and earned an Associate of Applied Science degree that allowed me to land an entry-level IT job. I again quickly moved through the levels as an IT professional, ultimately being promoted to management. The determined march to do more and more continued as I went back to college to receive a bachelor's in communication and a master's in counseling psychology.

As you can see, even while being pushed by my subconscious to do more for validation, my tendency to instinctively be a success-driven, hypervigilant, obsessive-compulsive perfectionist was actually serving me to improve myself and my position in the real world. I had become very comfortable with this personal identity and ego position of a successful leader while simultaneously carrying an internal rage. Most people never saw this rage within as it was mostly kept inside and only expressed verbally when I allowed it to see the light of day. After a while, I became aware that my internal rage was rooted in a lack of validation from my father. When I was about forty years old, I finally started to become expressly aware of my subconscious mind and the way it actually influenced my actions; the actions that I had thought were all the while under my conscious control. It was this moment of ego awareness that served as the catalyst for introspection, self-improvement work, growth, and healing.

Section 5.3—Evaluate How Well Your Needs Were Met

The next step in the process of rewriting our story is evaluating how well our basic needs were met in our early and later childhood years. As a basis for evaluating this, we actually need to look no further than Maslow's Hierarchy of Needs theory which is the inspiration for the base section of the Integrated Self Model. For this exercise, the question becomes: "How well were my needs met during the critical early foundational years of my life?"

Continuing with my story and considering the standard inventory of basic needs according to Maslow, which are food, shelter, safety, attachment, nurturing, validation, belonging, and self-esteem, it is important to note that at any stage of this exercise of writing and then rewriting our personal story, some deep emotions may come to the surface. Sit with these emotions for a while and reflect on the source experiences from which the emotions are birthed. Emotions are meant to be felt if we desire to release them and don't shy away from working with a mental health professional if you feel overwhelmed by these emotions. I will now briefly look at the individual basic needs and take note of how well these needs were met.

Subsistence (food, water, air, clothing, health, housing/shelter)—Overall, my basic needs were met in the area of subsistence. We lived in a mostly rural part of New York, about 75 miles north of New York City at the edge of a large apple orchard owned by my grandmother. The air was extremely clean and the environment was healthy, allowing for both physical and mental stimulation. The family home was small (about 1,200 square feet) but seemingly adequate for a family of six. I never felt crowded in the home, with the countryside readily available for physical separation and exploration.

As a family, we seemed to have enough food to eat as I don't recall ever feeling hungry; though I never really felt quite full (except for holiday dinners with extended family). Interestingly, I remember regularly eating mayonnaise-only and mayonnaise-and-ketchup sandwiches; however, this is a fond memory and not one of lack, at least not consciously. We did not have much money, but I do not recall anything negative about the need for clothing or shoes. My grandmother helped my parents with clothing for us and also paid for private Catholic school education.

Attachment (caregiver)—Overall, I believe that my basic needs were met in the area of attachment. I do not have any real memory of my very early childhood periods up to five years old. However, based partly on my perception of my early childhood experience, partly on my remembered later childhood experience, and partly on my all-too-well remembered, anxiously experienced adult relationships, it is my belief that, overall, my basic needs were met in this area in a very minimal manner. My mother spent all of her time at home as a stay-at-home mom and housewife. As an extreme introvert, my mother was not able to display emotions in any real, deep way. My mother always provided the required basic physical care for me and my siblings. She was not overtly caring, I guess; however, she was definitely not nurturing, at least not to me, personally.

With this said, my mother was consistent with the level of care and emotions shared. As such, this consistency allowed me to feel safe and secure with my mother, and even loved by her, in her own way. With this insight, I believe that this was how my mother operated as my caregiver in the earliest stages of my life. This stable, though moderated caregiver environment of having my basic physical needs met, while having my emotional needs neglected left me programmed to be predisposed to an anxious attachment style in adult relationships. My adult history of relationships including many broken hearts and two divorces, bears this out as being an accurate statement.

Safety / Certainty (physical, emotional)—Overall, my basic needs were met in the area of safety and certainty. Interestingly enough, when I considered the question of safety, my mind immediately focused the question on my feeling physically safe and did not consider emotional safety. Was this an honest omission, or was it a Freudian slip of exclusion? No matter, let's consider each.

Physical Safety: There was no physical or sexual abuse evident in the family, especially not in the core family home. I was only spanked once when I was six years old and it was not excessive at all. Excluding that one incident, there was no physical touch, neither observed nor experienced in the family home from my perspective. For the most part, there was not much tender, caring touch displayed in the family growing up; even hugs from my parents were rare for me as a child. My mother stayed home all of the time which made me feel safe and secure. Not only was my mother always home, but most of the houses on our street were occupied by close extended family members. I always felt safe in the neighborhood knowing that I was never more than a holler away from close family.

Emotional Safety: There were not any real overtly traumatic experiences to make me feel unsafe. The ebb and flow of the energy in the home was consistent. There was no alcohol or substance abuse, and no apparent mental health illnesses; nothing that would make me feel unsafe. Certainty (i.e., consistency) was probably *the* most positive quality of my childhood experience. Certainty provided a solid base on which to grow and launch, especially for my presumed *perfect* personality type as a child in this family.

Validation (self-confidence)—Based on the story of my childhood that I shared at the start of this exercise in taking the steps toward balance and growth, if I were to conclude that my basic needs were met in the area of validation, you could rightfully question my judgment. Honestly, with all things considered, my basic needs around validation were met, though maybe just minimally.

While I did carry deep father validation issues into my adult life, and while I struggled to heal the wounds and contain the internal rage fueled by emotional neglect, my self-confidence was extremely high. You may recall that as a twelve-year-old boy, I created the persona of a confident, capable, self-assured, extraverted individual for myself. This constructed persona was only able to work so effectively because it was actually propped up by an overwhelming level of validation that I had received from other sources like my grandmother, mother, aunts, and teachers (everyone else except for my father).

Reflecting further, my father never invalidated me. There was no criticism, shaming, or blaming from my father. He had merely failed to pay any explicit attention to me, apparently not knowing how to be a father to me. In retrospect, this lack of validation from my father coupled with the lack of invalidation from him was precisely what pushed me to create a confident persona and drive me to always be above average and successful in everything that I pursued.

Affection (nurturing)—The assessment of this basic need for affection is going to sound similar to the previous discussion of safety and certainty. As I said, there was no physical, caring, or tender touch displayed in the core family growing up. However, my grandmother and my aunt who lived nearby provided more than enough nurturing and care for me. They always seemed happy to see me, though my grandmother was on the stoic side, my aunt was openly loving and demonstrative. While I developed validation issues from the lack of interconnection, communication, and affection explicitly from my father, I experienced enough love, affection, and nurturing from my mother and other extended family members.

Belonging (wanted)—Even though I was not nurtured within my core family structure, I consider that my basic needs were met in the area of belonging. Even though I felt invisible, I can honestly say that I did feel that I was part of a family, nonetheless. My father went to work every day, leaving and returning at the same time. My mother was always home providing basic levels of care, a clean home, and dinner on the table at the same time every night.

My paternal grandmother, aunt, and uncle were constantly stopping by, modeling what a family looked like for me. The Diorio family holiday meals involved about twenty relatives gathered around the dinner table filled with jokes, stories, laughter, traditions, and good memories. In addition, we would have visits with my aunt, uncle, and close cousins each week and for each child's birthday.

I never considered belonging, or more specifically not belonging, as an issue for most of my life. Upon reflection, it was only during my adolescent years that I began to consciously feel myself to be very different from my core family members; that there was something not quite congruent with who I knew was inside and how the family operated in life. However, the sense of separateness from my family only existed within myself and my mind as I got older into my teenage years and beyond. I started understanding how unhealthy and dysfunctional the core family system was.

Self-esteem/significance (valued)—This is one main area of basic needs that causes me to scratch my head in wonder and amazement. I do not understand how I could possibly grow up with high self-esteem having experienced such a lack of validation from my parents. Apparently, it was the lack of explicit invalidation that allowed me to be so strongly supportive of myself. No one spoke to me, at least not much; so there was no one overtly telling me that I was not good enough, stupid, wrong, or a failure. These implicit messages did get planted in my subconscious mind and eventually impacted my way of thinking once I reached adulthood.

As a young child, I was very curious about and very interested in nature and how the world operated. I would investigate and analyze everything that crossed my field of vision and perception. I would easily attempt to do things without the fear of failure or the fear of being corrected. Trial-and-error was a very natural and normal state of being in the world for me. I was never alone, with the awareness that there was a God who would watch over me and to whom I prayed for help when I found myself in a nervous situation like when I took apart my father's electric razor to see how it worked but then struggled to put it back together without my parents finding out.

With this experience of wonder and adventure as a young child, I can now understand why I would create a persona for myself of a confident, capable, outgoing person, and how I could so easily and successfully move forward in my life wearing this remarkable suit of confidence. This relatively protected childhood, along with the validation and accolades from my teachers, provided me with all the necessary tools to start and perpetuate an extremely high level of confidence and self-esteem. Being alone to take care of myself also allowed me to not have anyone else's voice in my head besides my own to debate my thoughts, actions, and decisions. Experiencing solitude and even isolation as a young child through my teenage years turned out to be a literal blessing in disguise.

When I look at the Integrated Self Model and consider the whole of my personal story, I think about the inventory of basic needs. When I reflect on this aspect of my life through my own remembered experience, my first impression is that overall, my basic needs were met during my childhood years. If I pause for a moment, however, to allow myself to go deeper to touch the truth of it all, I actually find that my basic needs were satisfied (barely) but satisfied enough to provide a somewhat stable base upon which to build my life.

This discovery that my basic needs were met during childhood understandably played a huge role in how I was able to effectively reinvent my identity when I was about twelve years old, and then successfully launch myself into my teenage and adult years. The fact that my basic needs were just barely met during my formative years means (1) my basic needs were met, and (2) my basic needs were barely met, as a constant reminder that with one slip up or mistake, it could mean that I could be poor, hungry, neglected, without love, and so forth. It was this sense of only having the bare minimum and the threat of losing it all if I stopped pushing myself even for a moment to take a breath, that motivated me to be what some may call an overachiever, or a type A personality. I could not and would not stop to rest as I had experientially learned that I was essentially alone in this world and had to take care of myself.

Section 5.4—Evaluate Significant Early Relationships

When we discuss our early significant relationships, we are mainly talking about our parents and core family that lived in the same household as we did. However, these relationships may actually reach beyond our immediate family for some of us. For this discussion, we will include the primary and secondary caregivers, extended family, and those in positions of trust. We will focus on these significant relationships during the early childhood years from birth to seven years old, and then also include later childhood years from seven to twelve years old.

The quality of our primary caregivers in the first eighteen months of life is critical to the development of healthy attachments. In this initial early childhood period, the primary caregiver relationship must be steady, consistent, responsive, caring, and nurturing to provide a sense of safety to the newborn child, which results in the development of a secure attachment. If this healthy caretaking environment is not experienced by the newborn child, an insecure attachment is developed. The insecure attachments are anxious, avoidant, and disorganized. Anxious-insecure attachment occurs when the caregiver is inconsistent, providing a sense of safety and care at times, but not at other times. Avoidant-insecure attachment is developed when the caregiver consistently does not adequately respond to the needs of the child and is not able to be accepting of the child. Disorganized-insecure attachment in the child is commonly caused by childhood trauma, neglect, and fear as the child sees the caregiver as both the source of comfort and the source of fear.

Even when the quality of our primary caregivers in the first eighteen months of life is considered healthy and secure, an unhealthy attachment can still be established and entrenched in the child after eighteen months during the remainder of the early childhood period, obviously depending on the quality of primary and secondary experiences by the child. However, an unhealthy attachment developed during the first eighteen months will not be healed and resolved in the subsequent early childhood years. Regardless of when the insecure attachment is developed during the early childhood years from birth to seven years old, the insecure attachment will be carried into adulthood and experienced until it is hopefully addressed. These insecure attachments from early childhood will present as insecure attachments in adulthood.

Anxious-attachment and avoidant-attachment styles are commonly found matched up in relationships as we try to work through the insecure attachment wounds as adults. Unfortunately, insecure attachment issues from childhood are best addressed through therapy outside the stress of a relationship, though couples therapy can be effective if both partners are committed to the relationship and agree to do the necessary work in addressing and healing the insecure attachment issues.

Regarding my own attachment experience in my early childhood, my mother was my primary caregiver who was always present and consistent in providing a safe and stable environment for me during the first eighteen months. However, it is my memory that my mother was not emotionally available to me (or others). She had always been private, reserved, and not nurturing at all for the remainder of my childhood and teenage years. My needs were met, but barely so. In my early adult relationships before much self-improvement work and healing, I displayed evidence of an anxious attachment style by entering into romantic relationships with women who were emotionally unavailable and whose attention and affection fluctuated on and off. My relationship with my father was nonexistent even though my father was present around the home day to day. He seemed to be of a similar personality to my mother where no emotions by the children were allowed in the home, and only adults expressed emotions of annoyance, disapproval, and anger. My father acted in charge, but my mother was the head of the household who told my dad what to do. We learned quickly that the best way to keep from receiving a scolding was to stay away from each other and to remain quiet. There was no physical violence, only stress and the threat of loud scolding, disapproval, and anger.

Next, as I consider my relationships with extended family, I warmly remember most of these relationships being constant sources of attention, nurturing, and love. My fraternal grandmother and aunt were a few houses away and were my favorite people in my life growing up. Even my other aunts, uncles, and maternal grandparents were positive influences on me which supplemented and mostly offset the lack of empathy, attention, and nurturing from my primary caregivers. With my mother staying at home the majority of the time, other significant relationships such as teachers and coaches, and my extended family, I felt I received a supportive and positive influence on me that sort of diluted the lack of validation and attention from my parents.

Section 5.5—Identify Your Core Childhood Issues

The next thing for us to consider is: "What are the core issues, identities, and characteristics that we carried out of the early childhood years that essentially programmed us how to be, feel, and act? It might be quite obvious to those of you who have been working on self-development and diving into this work to heal your inner child. For those of you who have not quite yet gotten to this conversation, I will now work through the list of some common core childhood issues that I experienced.

People-Pleaser: It is very common to hear the words "people-pleaser" or the phrase "people-pleasing tendencies." When you are not getting validation from your parents, family, or friends through being complimented, encouraged, seen, recognized, and valued, you start to search for those feelings through other means to earn the validation and love that you need. Looking back, I can easily see my behaviors that were indications of being a people-pleaser. Even though we did not have chores to do, I clearly remember doing things to help my mother such as ironing clothes. To be clear, I did not do this often, but just enough to test the theory that this would earn my mother's validation. I am assuming that this did not result in explicit validation from my mother, otherwise, I would've done more ironing and chores for her. Nonetheless, my sisters called me "goody-two-shoes," which was a popular expression of disdain in the 1960s.

Perfectionism: Another way to gain validation was by being perfect at everything that I did. I would try my hardest to get the best grades, be quiet and obedient, and always look for ways to gain attention and validation from my parents. When being a people-pleaser was not fully effective in the attempt to earn love, I had to do things better. Naturally, I came to understand that I needed to act perfectly, get perfect grades, and never make mistakes, in order to earn love and validation from my father. The truth of the matter is I am now sure that my father did love me, though he did not know how to express or communicate that love and affection. My father's father died in a farming accident when my father was thirteen years old.

Apparently, he was never validated as a child himself and my father's relationship with his father was probably quiet and reserved having grown up in the 1920s and 1930s.

Lack of validation: Seemingly, my father's relationship with me was not a conscious decision and judgment of me. In the end, he is not to be faulted for his failure to validate me; however, for me as a young son naturally seeking his approval and not receiving it created deep childhood wounds that I would carry for decades. Even though this was not his direct fault, my father gets no credit for being a good father, though maybe some credit for working hard, not getting violent or addicted to substances, and providing a roof over our heads. Oddly, my relationship with my mother was similar to my father, but I did not carry deep wounds from her. I suspect that, since my mother was home all of the time, I received just enough attention for it to not result in the way it had with my father. As a male child, I also suspect that validation from the same-gender parent was paramount to me, and helped form my prevailing childhood issues around validation to my father.

Fear of Being Seen: As a people-pleaser, I did not want to upset either of my parents or displease them. Anything with regard to being noticed or seen would bring displeasure and annoyance to my parents, which was the opposite of what I sought. Being in people-pleaser mode all of the time meant that this other side of the coin issue of getting the wrong kind of attention was quite scary for me and it developed into a fear of being noticed, recognized, or seen.

Hypervigilance: In order to keep from annoying or upsetting my parents, I would closely and obsessively watch how people moved around the house. I would observe the tone of every conversation and try to determine if someone was in a good mood or a bad mood. This extreme-observer behavior is known as hypervigilance, which resulted in me being very reactive to any negative stimulus that was going on in the home, or even potential negative stimulus. Even the smallest of things being out of place might cause someone to get angry.

Fear of being unseen/Fear of being insignificant: I mentioned how, as a child, I had the fear of being seen; however, the flipside as being the fear of not being seen is also real at the same time. We all have the fear of not being seen by the people most important to us, starting with our parents. For me, what if, as a self-identified invisible child, my parents were never able to see me, really see me? Would I matter to someone/anyone? Would I be insignificant? Would I even exist at all? This is why, at twelve years old, I created the external persona to allow me to be publicly seen, while my inner child self was able to remain safely unseen.

Emotional Neglect: While there was no physical violence or sexual abuse in my experience growing up, there were no acts of connection, nurturing, caring, or kindness expressed. Feelings were not allowed in the home unless it was expressed by my father. I shared earlier that my one and only spanking was when I was about six years old because I was crying, which taught me that feelings were not allowed and there would be consequences for expressing my feelings.

Money Beliefs: There was one more thing that significantly impacted my adult life subconsciously. We did not have much money growing up, though my parents put on the pretense that we did. Eventually, I realized in my adult years that I had brought this feeling of not being worthy to have money from my childhood and that I was carrying these limiting beliefs and thoughts about money. Even though we did not have much money growing up, my father would have fresh Italian bread at every meal, a special brand-name ginger ale that was delivered by truck each week, and he even bought a brand new speedboat when I was a teenager. To add to my mindset around money and not being valued, I remember going to school in seventh grade with a hole at the bottom of my shoe and my foot being soaking wet. Besides feeling embarrassed, this whole situation begged the question, "Why do I have to go to school with a hole in the bottom of my shoes while my father got all of this extra stuff?"

Not Feeling Valued: From the perspective of a very young child, the answer to this mostly rhetorical question of "Why did my father get extra and I got less?" was that I am not valued by my parents, I am not worthy to have money or the things that money provides. This experience taught me that needing a new pair of shoes was less important than my father's need to drink a special ginger ale and eat his fresh Italian bread at every meal. Even today, I cannot intellectually argue with this conclusion I came to at a very young age. This conclusion of my younger Self easily got etched in my brain's neural pathways and emotionally stored in my mind and body. This is why it takes conscious effort to address and heal early childhood wounds, and why most people remain under the influence of their childhood experience most of their lives.

Today I appreciate my siblings' experiences more now that I understand my own experiences and how they affected me. I have come to conclude during my adult years that I probably had it the easiest of all my siblings and I mean that sincerely. In my perception growing up, everyone in the family received the same treatment, so no one sibling was the favorite or received special treatment. I do remember stories that my siblings would share in my adult years, believing that I received better treatment compared to them, but to me and my own experience, I had received the same treatment as they had. There was definitely something not quite right going on there in our family system back then.

The subconscious push for me to be perfect in order to gain my father's validation and love began to unravel during my freshman year in high school. One day, I brought my report card home eager to show it to my father. Cheering to myself inside, "I did it! I finally did it!" I had received a 100 percent in mathematics and was absolutely sure that this perfect grade would earn my father's approval. When he came home from work, I positioned myself in front of him beaming with pride and proudly presented the report card to him. My father said, and I quote, "Why can't you do that all the time?" in a rhetorical tone, not wanting me to answer. I now understand that in his own underdeveloped parental mind, my father had meant this as encouragement for me to keep striving for the perfect grade, for perfectionism.

Finally, the subconscious spell pushing me to obsessively work to earn my father's validation was broken for my conscious mind. However, the wound had already been programmed deeply within my inner child and subconscious mind, which was tightly set to be a people-pleaser, a perfectionist, and hypervigilant. While consciously giving up any expectation of ever being able to earn his love and approval, subconsciously I remained unchanged. Without a conscious outlet, this unfulfilled need for validation grew into an internal rage as an adult.

In summary, here are the childhood wounds I carried into my adult years:

1. Insecure Attachment: Resulting in an anxious attachment style in relationships.
2. Emotional Neglect: Emotional expression was not encouraged, and nurturing was not present making connections superficial.
3. Lack of Validation from my parents: Praise and encouragement were not expressed to me which resulted in feeling like I needed to continue to overachieve.
4. People-Pleaser: Taking action on things around the house for my parents hoping they would show praise, approval, or gratitude to me.
5. Perfectionist: If I did everything to the best of my ability maybe my parents would love me more.
6. Hypervigilant: I can stay safe if I watch others carefully and predict what will happen.
7. Fear of Being Seen/Unseen: Being seen means trouble, being unseen means no validation.
8. Limiting Beliefs—Worthiness: I am not worthy or valued. I do not deserve material things.
9. Limiting Beliefs—Money: I am not valued/valuable. Others deserve money more than I do.
10. Limiting Beliefs—Money: Money is the root of all evil. Only bad/ruthless people have lots of money.

Here are some other childhood wounds that you may have developed and healed during your adult experiences:

- Parent(s) had mental illness: Depression, anxiety, bipolar disorder, borderline personality disorder, narcissism

- Parent(s) had addiction: drugs, alcohol, gambling, sex
- Limiting Beliefs—Money: poverty, homelessness, welfare, generational poverty
- Anxiety from Trauma: caused by sexual abuse/assault, physical abuse/assault, abandonment, fear
- Physical Disability: para/quadriplegic, muscular dystrophy, blindness, mutism, deafness
- Mental Illness: depression, anxiety, bipolar disorder, PTSD, personality disorder, narcissism
- Mental Challenges: down syndrome, brain injury, cerebral palsy, neurodivergence
- Health Challenges: premature birth, diagnosed with disease or disorder in childhood

Section 5.6—Assess Current State of Ego Development

Going through this process of assessing your state of ego development can actually be the catalyst for advancement by bringing a thought from the subconscious mind to the conscious mind. The birth of a human child has always been perceived by most as the greatest gift of all miracles on earth. This miraculous event that marks the innovation of the human-spirit life also marks the activation of the ego's subconscious mind to focus on the survival of the human-spirit Self.

Your experience of the ego development process will not be the same as others because it will be viewed and experienced through the lens of your personal identity, state of existence, personal experiences, and whether your mindset is rooted in lack/scarcity, or abundance/faith. From the moment of incarnation, our ego is focused on protecting the Self. The Soul is mostly asleep at the start of our human-spirit existence, and though not aware of the Soul at this point, the Ego is keeping the Soul safe while it waits for its awakening to begin its evolution and journey back to Source.

When considering our current state of ego development for this exercise, it is important to identify key milestones of your specific ego development. These key milestones are points in your life when your

Ego reaches significant moments of awareness. Previously, I shared my personal story from birth through my teenage years into adulthood. For this exercise, let's use the age of eighteen years old as the starting point of my ego development process. Up until that time, my ego identity was being formed through mostly unconscious programming of nature, nurture, trauma, basic needs, and trial-and-error.

Though each person will have their own unique experience, my ego awareness seemed to switch on when I entered the real world of self-preservation and self-survival (around eighteen years of age) marked by both my graduation from high school and my first full-time job as a stock clerk. While the basic ego development process had begun at this point, my conscious awareness was mostly undeveloped, mostly unaware, relying on the subconscious mind and its programming to move me through life. All of my actions were driven by my childhood experiences and the resulting core childhood wounds (identified earlier). One mitigating factor for the impact of these identified issues on my adult life was the fact that I had constructed a strong, confident, outgoing persona to embody going forward when I was in sixth grade. This constructed persona took care of most of my childhood wounds by keeping my inner child feeling safe. I used the intense, anxious push of my inner child fear to remain safe as my superpower for achievement, advancement, and impetus in every aspect of my adult life.

While most of my childhood wounds were kept at bay by the construction of an external persona, my validation wound left an anger unaddressed inside of me that grew into an internal rage. This anger resided close to the surface, appearing quickly to defend myself whenever I felt anything less than perfect or valued. The internal rage stayed mostly dormant but ready to erupt to protect my honor, like the Incredible Hulk. Fortunately, my internal rage came out verbally and not physical violence; however, every eruption was accompanied by embarrassment and shame. I knew that this anger was out of control and out of my control which let me know that I had to change.

I believe the turning point for me was when I chose to move with my job and my own family (wife and children) about two thousand miles away from my family of origin at the age of thirty-three. This was a natural, subtle cut-off from the same people and unhealthy environment that produced and sustained my inner child wounds. This increased physical distance and the added duration between visits back *home* allowed me to take several breaths and begin to heal. The hard work of addressing my inner child wounds began organically for me, and gradually took hold.

I started my inner child healing through self-reflection and self-improvement books but the initial catalyst for my personal growth came from my IT job in the form of a Myers-Briggs Type Indicator (MBTI) personality test and assessment. I will explain this event in more detail in a later section; however, let it suffice to say that the MBTI test revealed to me that I needed to be and wanted to be a better human being; less of a robot and more of a caring person. At that moment, I was determined to start feeling more. This was a solid start to my personal growth and to my ego development, but there was so much more to uncover and heal.

My inner child wounds were very deep, as most childhood wounds are until they were uncovered through deliberate and targeted mental health treatment. Throughout this healing process, I found that childhood trauma and wounds are experienced as forms of shame and guilt, which are the lowest levels of energy and vibration reflected as such on the Map of Consciousness (covered later in this book). To focus on my anger, rage, and other wounds, I turned to several books by John Bradshaw such as *Healing the Shame That Binds You*[37] and *Creating Love*,[38] among others.

Once I had begun making significant inroads to healing my inner child wounds, I started to expand my vision and reach from an exclusively internal world to a world that included some external interactions. I became aware of the book, *The Four Agreements*[39] and I began living my life in accordance with the wise guidance offered, namely (1) Be Impeccable with Your Word, (2) Don't Take Anything Personally, (3) Don't Make Assumptions, and (4) Always Do Your Best. These *agreements* became my personal commitments and my daily mantras. By taking this aligned action and committing to this personal growth and change, my Ego became more and more in balance with my Soul, moving me toward contentment and peace.

At the same time, I began working on my interpersonal relationships including my relations with romantic partners. The anxious-attachment style that I developed in childhood attracted me to romantic partners with an avoidant-attachment style. I was destined to keep repeating these insecure attachment relationships until I was able to heal my inner child attachment issues and choose relationships based on a secure attachment. To focus on my tendency of codependency and understand how to cultivate healthy relationships, I read the book *Conscious Loving*.[40]

The road to healing the inner child wounds for me wasn't easy; it required self-honesty and committing to a new and conscious way of living. As much as the mental health discussion is still not a mainstream topic, it was much less supported forty years ago, especially for a man. This mental health journey would essentially continue through the earning of my master's degree in counseling psychology. This significant ego development milestone exactly coincided with my spiritual evolution, resulting in increasing balance and expanding consciousness. At that time, I still had some limiting beliefs and attachment wounds to work on; however, for the most part, I had become a mentally healthy, functioning human being who was also spiritually awake and evolved.

Of all the childhood traumas and wounds that I worked through, I believe that this wound of insecure attachment was the most impactful for me. It always required another person for me to be able to work on and through my attachment issues. The unconscious relationships with my parents resulted in the unintended consequence of looking for love in all the wrong places, with all the *wrong* people. Without these relationships that didn't work out, I would still be feeling unloved as they pushed me to love myself. Somehow, I was able to find my way through the forest of children masquerading as adults, some even as healthy adults carrying a lifetime of hurt, disappointment, and failed relationships.

In the words of Spiritual Coach Jennifer Hargis,

> I think for so many of us we've received such inconsistent pockets of love and affection

> growing up that we have created this persona, this image, subconsciously throughout our life… and it's all in an effort to be more appetizing to those around us. You wake up as an adult and you don't know who you are. And we thought making friends as an adult was hard. Try getting to know yourself. But what are these cascading impacts of having lived a life in this false persona for so long… It means you've likely spent a life molding your character around what others wanted you to be in all circumstances, in every nuance, in every situation… with a series of toxic relationships that likely went right alongside them. We can really boil all of this down, all of the pain and the trauma that we carry around inside ourselves unhealed year over year, is the crying of our authentic self wanting to get out; that light that is buried under all that heavy darkness is screaming at you now, at this stage of your life… and you feel for the first time that maybe you're ready to tackle it but you're stuck. You are entering the dark night of the soul, which is truly the period of your shadow work, where your subconscious mind is starting to examine all of the dark shadows that exist in your personality and brings them to the surface so they can get a little bit of light.[41]

Author Michael Singer in the book *The Untethered Soul* offers for us to consider,

> There is nothing more important to true growth than realizing that you are not the voice in your mind—you are the one that hears it. If you don't understand this, you will try to figure out which of the many things the voice says is

> really you. People go through so many changes in the name of 'trying to find myself.' They want to discover which of these voices, which of these aspects of their personality, is who they really are. The answer is simple: none of them.[42]

During some periods of your life, you will think that it would be much easier to just let your undeveloped ego control your actions and reactions, and keep running the unconscious programming of your childhood wounds in a loop without the constant struggle of doing what feels right or what is best for you. However, you will never have true peace if you're constantly forced to heal with your unconscious reactions to life events, stressors, and unplanned curve-balls. While healing your inner child wounds takes courage, bravery, and conscious effort, it is all worth it in the end for you to break the chains from the wounds that bind you to experience peace, a life in flow, and your authentic Self.

Section 5.7—Assess Current State of Soul Evolution

If the invocation of the human-spirit existence at birth is the greatest miracle (marking the activation of the human Ego's subconscious mind and the potentiality of reconnection with the Source), then the second greatest miracle is the moment of the awakening of the human Soul that carries the echoes of the Divine Spirit, the memories of Source, even though initially only experienced by the human Self as a vague emptiness. The same as with your experience of your ego and its development, the experience of your Soul awakening and its subsequent evolution will not be the same for each person because the catalyst for this awakening is not certain, not guaranteed, and the timing varies when it finally does occur.

Without the awakening of the Soul, the human-spirit experience will remain mostly one-sided (in respect to the Model), and one-dimensional with the focus of the subconscious mind on survival and on the development of the ego, in the best of circumstances. In the worst of circumstances, the focus of the subconscious mind will be exclusively on survival, and any real development of the Ego beyond survival will be foregone; the need to awaken the Soul is put out of the mind. Without the awakening of the Soul at some point during the human lifetime, the person will remain out of balance, and will most likely experience a lifetime of some level of internal confusion and unexplainable, undeniable angst.

Many times the human Soul will be awakened by a tragic experience, and often it is when the Ego becomes aware of its own mortality which results in a curiosity and the search for something beyond this lifetime. This occurs even with deeply religious people who spent a lifetime following religion without ever questioning the institution's dogma (essential teachings, absolute law) and doctrines (firmly established guidelines, subject to interpretation), without the doubting that will normally serve to strengthen their long-held religious beliefs, or that will lead to the establishment of their own personal tapestry of a spiritual belief system.

As for myself, who was consistently exposed to the existence of God and Jesus through growing up in a devout Catholic family, including *religiously* going to Mass every Sunday and attending the parish Catholic elementary school from first to eighth grade, I was always spiritually aware, though I would not say that I was spiritually awake during my childhood. From very early on, I did not accept that God was an angry, punitive, vengeful God who was always ready to smite sinners and send them to hell for eternity. My God (the Father) was a loving God, and Jesus was always seen as a role model to me. Considering my unique, personal situation, we can say that I was born into a human-spirit Self with a vague spiritual awareness. You will see that even being somewhat spiritually aware, the awakening of my Soul was not hastened, and this situation may have even delayed the Soul's awakening. Without an actual awakening of the soul, the evolution of the Soul will be impeded, delayed, or even nonexistent in some cases.

Up until the moment of my actual spiritual awakening, I had a strong relationship with God. I self-identified as a Catholic even well into my twenties, and then as a nondenominational Christian. Thinking about it now, I must have believed that my locus of control was external to me; however, I never felt a lack of control in my world. I believed that all I needed to do was ask God through sincere prayer and it was done. This was an unusual perspective as typically, most people who had an external locus of control would feel that things happened to them in the world. For me, I believed that things happened for me, and for my highest good. For whatever reason, I believed that I was favored by God, my Father.

I had no explanation of how or why this would be true but I never had a reason to question it. I did one day come to wonder why God would favor me so much and protect me from harm. At that moment, I was "told" that I was a son of God, that we all are literally children of God. I instantly began sobbing in gratitude, knowing that this was true, and always has been. At this moment, my locus of control came to live within me, all the while knowing that Source was the source of the power that I now personally possess, which is shared by all of God's children. With this knowledge, some would say that I had a spiritual awakening but at a smaller magnitude of realization compared to later in my life.

I would like to contend that I did not fully start to awaken until about the age of forty-five years old. Up to that point, I had lived a good life and considered myself a *good* person. However, I was seemingly living in a trance. During that time, there was very little separation between my conscious mind and my subconscious mind. I was thinking, feeling, and making decisions according to my subconscious programming and acting in accordance with my lived experiences as a child. However, I did not fully wake up to the whole spiritual scene until I was about fifty years old and I began working on some of the last limiting beliefs that I held since childhood.

Thirty years ago, I finally awakened spiritually, unaware that this seemingly ordinary day would somehow activate my spiritual awakening and would forever be such a significant milestone in my life and a moment that I would think back on many times in wonder over my lifetime. While I had already begun my ego development, moving well toward self-awareness, this definitely was not a conscious decision to awaken spiritually. This is where divine inspiration and divine intervention seemed to have teamed up to move me beyond that brink, to the rediscovery of my Soul.

One summer day in the mid-1990s, I was working on my son's car in the garage of our home. As a new driver, my son had a car accident and I was repairing the damaged fender. Though I do not recall having ever done so before this day, I had set up a television in the garage to keep me company and entertained. On this particular day, I found myself watching Oprah Winfrey's show where she interviewed author James Redfield about his book, *The Celestine Prophecy*,[43] neither of which I heard of previously.

Redfield was talking about his book with Oprah, and to this day, I can't even tell you what was actually said about the book that ended up catching my attention and interest. How the book found its way into my hands is a mystery. Once I picked up the book, I found it to be an easy read and it lit a spark in me. From then and there, I started growing spiritually, studying and exploring its contents.

As I read, the magic of this hidden spiritual world was revealed to me through parables, slowly so that I would not be frightened away. This book, *The Celestine Prophecy*, would go on to open my eyes and Soul to the small, unseen miracles that are sprinkled over us each and every day by Source to support us during our human-spirit experience. The very first golden nugget of magic presented in the book was that, if we had a question in our mind, we only had to hold it consciously and Source would send the answer to us through seemingly chance encounters and experiences. For me, this was a sign that God was indeed watching over us and that my angels were always there to support and guide me whenever I needed. Understanding that this spiritual guidance is always available was very interesting and calming to know. I now think that this was not the most valuable gift from the book.

The story posed a rather benign question to the main character of the book. When you look at the world, at nature, specifically the trees, what do you see? Do you see the tree as a flat, two-dimensional painting? Or do you see the tree in its true three-dimensional beauty? I was utterly surprised, even shocked by my own answer to this query. Of course, I am seeing the world in three dimensions, but I found that I definitely was not seeing the natural beauty and essence of the living things in the world. With a little practice, I started becoming aware of a three-dimensional world that had been hiding from me in plain sight all of this time. What a gift!

Without giving an entire synopsis of this book, let it suffice to say that a world full of magic, wonderment, potentiality, and spirituality was placed at my feet. I only had to pick this gift up and claim it for myself. The existence of auras, energy, and vibrations was revealed to me along with an understanding of how humans unconsciously compete for energy if operating from our subconscious programming. In my opinion, *The Celestine Prophecy*, along with the previously mentioned book, The Four Agreements,[44] are together *the* most significant sources of practical information to help move a person toward balanced personal and spiritual growth.

Once I awakened spiritually, my Soul yearned to evolve and grow closer to God. Guided by divine inspirations and synchronicities, I was presented with book after book, each appearing at the moment that I held the question. These books did not teach me what to believe but rather appeared to offer validation (and comfort) to me for what I had already come to suspect as being my new truth of it all. The book *Conversations with God, Book 1*[45] came to me next, seemingly as a way to build a bridge for me between this world of pain and hardship and the spiritual world of miracles as a way to resolve my questions and confusions birthed by my Catholic teachings. This book provided an acceptable preface for my personal story, a reasonable explanation for why we were incarnated here on Earth. Further, it offered explanations for many of the things that I had wondered about as a Catholic person. I knew consciously that this book was a story, but much of its contents seemed believable to me. Much of the book gave me the bricks to continue to build a firm foundation of beliefs on which to construct the evolving whole of my personal belief system.

As a self-identified *scientist* who requires ample evidence of something before I accept any claims as fact, I spent the next few years curiously observing and testing each theory, especially the one that would deliver the answer to me as I held the question or intention. The real-life evidence supporting the varied metaphysical and spiritual claims mounted and I eventually found myself looking for a spiritual connection that was rooted in love and only in love. In other words, I was looking for a Source in this world of competing religions and religious leaders who were literally banging on their pulpits in righteousness, delivering messages of fear, punishment, fire, and brimstone to keep the flock coming back for a connection to Source.

In 2003, after not finding what I was seeking at a Christian church, the trail of spiritual breadcrumbs led me to a New Thought church that embraced the true spirit of Jesus Christ. This church offered a sanctuary of unconditional love, acceptance, and inclusion both spiritually and literally without the threat of eternal damnation. Immediately, I knew without a doubt that I found my spiritual home where the senior minister's sermons and teachings focused on love and being human in this world by offering alternative ways of being, doing, and acting through individual choice and in support of each person's unique individual and spiritual path.

The deeply spiritual, loving energy of this New Thought church attracted several highly profiled, well-known guest speakers to appear in person at the church. During my time attending this church from 2003 to 2010, I had the very special honor and privilege to attend in-person speaking events with Wayne Dyer, Deepak Chopra, Louise Hay, David Hawkins, and Marianne Williamson (to name only a few). Dyer and Chopra became regular speakers at the church and to this day I still consider them my personal spiritual guides and mentors.

When I attended my first spiritual event at this church, it was to see and listen to Wayne Dyer as he shared his ideas and teachings from his latest inspirational book, *The Power of Intention*.[46] Wayne Dyer's words lit me up from the inside out. I must have been glowing because the person sitting next to me leaned over to me during the presentation and said, "You know what he is talking about, don't you?" Yes, yes, I did. Wayne Dyer was speaking the truth of what I had recently come to know. In the next five years or so, Dyer would come back to the New Thought church several times, as he himself continued to evolve spiritually.

During this same time period, Deepak Chopra came to speak at the church several times. I had already been introduced to his wonderful book, *The Seven Spiritual Laws of Success*,[47] as well as others. Chopra and Dyer became my role models of what it was to be a spiritual being having a human experience. They were both strong and soft, confident and humble, divine and human, all at the same time. They were living the way that I had always envisioned Jesus to have walked on the Earth. They both embodied the ways of Jesus, each in their own way, walking among us as if we were the same as they were.

In this divinely inspirational and loving environment, my Soul continued to evolve exponentially, especially while I was also doing the difficult work of healing my inner child wounds as part of the ego development process. My Soul and Ego first gradually and then more quickly came into balance, and my spiritual Self seemingly began to grow to a point I never experienced before. I did not understand what was happening, although I knew it was good and divinely guided.

Even though I was not seeking an explanation, the answer was provided to me. The book *Power vs. Force* by David Hawkins came into my conscious mind and my hands. I devoured the contents of that book, with a particular interest and focus on the Levels of Consciousness. I came to understand that my growing spirituality and growing sense of contentment that I was experiencing was explained as expanded consciousness. As my Ego development came into balance with my Soul's evolution, my Ego began to cooperate with my Soul in partnership and my level of vibration continued to increase. In other words, my level of consciousness continued to expand. It was no real surprise when David Hawkins came to my church to speak during the time I was reading *Power vs. Force*, and I no longer became surprised by these *coincidences* that I had only come to know as divine support.

The evolution of my Soul continued for a few more years, peaking and then leveling out at a relatively high level of consciousness. The milestone of my Soul's evolution coincided with a corresponding milestone of my Ego's development with the completion of my master's degree in counseling psychology, having sufficiently healed my inner child wounds enough to enjoy the contentment and peace brought about by my expanding consciousness.

Now that I am at this advanced position in my Soul's evolution where I have come to experience love, joy, and peace in my day-to-day life more times than not, I am able to take a breath and wonder about that moment of awakening. What was it that shook my Soul gently to create a stirring that would cause me to move from a spiritual awareness to become spiritually awakened and to be the catalyst for my Soul's evolution?

As profoundly summed up by Spiritual Coach Jennifer Hargis,

> What does it mean to be spiritual? It means that I acknowledge that I'm more than just a shell. I'm more than just a physical body… that I have a soul and a higher self, and I have a spiritual energy to me that far exceeds what you see in front of you. An awakening is an awareness, a new awareness, to a notion or idea, in this case a reality, but to say that one is spiritually awakened means that you have become aware of your Higher Self. In church you listen to people tell you all the time that you have a soul that lives inside of you, but I think a lot of us just feel like it's our personality. It's your life event that has caused you to hit rock bottom. What this trauma does is it ignites shadow work. Shadow work is the process of connecting emotional triggers that you experience in your life today to past trauma. Once you start to see the connectedness to everything in your life, it blows the roof right off. Start living from a place of gratitude… Gratitude for me now is my spiritual awakening. Gratitude now has shown me how special I am, and that I have a place in this universe just like you do. What spiritual awakening has shown me is that

> there is no such thing as separateness. It's where the gratitude stems from.[48]

Without a spiritual awakening, without the moment when the fog lifted, when I could finally see clearly and feel deeply, the advanced evolution of my Soul would not have been realized; at least not yet, and maybe not even in this lifetime. It all starts with a spiritual awakening, with the awareness of a personal Soul, and with an awareness of Source.

Section 5.8—Assess your Level of Consciousness

According to the model and framework, the extent of our internal confusion, conflict, anxiety, stress, struggle, and angst may be observed and assessed as the degree to which the Ego and Soul have (or have not) come into balance and integrated. In the model, this degree of integration can be directly interpreted as the individual's current level of consciousness, as described by David R. Hawkins, MD, PhD in his book, *Power vs. Force: The Hidden Determinants of Human Behavior.*

Before going further down this path, we want to have a straightforward conversation about the levels of consciousness, what they mean, and how to use the information. While the levels of consciousness are represented by a table of values and meaningful words, it is important that you understand the overall intention and context of this information. It would be so easy for us to take hold of only those elements of the table and the levels of consciousness that support our current suspicions or existing beliefs, the elements that will make us feel good about ourselves, and that can be used to convince ourselves (or others) that we are okay, maybe even doing better than others. Yes, we are human, and our egos are constantly craving any indication that we are okay, and that will feed our insecurities.

First, let's take a breath, connect with Source, get still, and be discerning. You always have a chance to choose what is useful and meaningful to you, what to believe, and what to eventually know to be your truth. The defined levels seem to imply that a higher level of consciousness is better than another. While embodying a higher level of consciousness through integration will bring you increasing levels of personal power, contentment, love, and peace, there are challenges, lessons, and growth to be experienced on the other levels. If you can become proficient at using these levels of consciousness to understand your current state, support your healing and growth, and meet yourself wherever you are in life, you will have a roadmap to navigate through the lower levels of consciousness and be able to move toward higher levels of acceptance, love, joy, and peace.

Second, it is necessary to be discerning and to understand the intent (or heart) of the author, any author, and to understand the context for the information being gathered and shared. For this author, David Hawkins, his intentions and context for his book were made clear by him in the preface of *Power vs. Force*.

> While the truths reported in this book were scientifically derived and objectively organized, like all truths, they were first experienced, personally... Follow this fascinating journey and you'll see how easy it can be to raise your consciousness to levels of power, rather than force, so that you can become one of those who is awake and aware in this world. Your life will certainly never be the same.[49]

In lieu of stopping right now to read his powerful book, I will summarize the basic elements of the table from the book for you, and then provide a brief explanation of how you might view the information and how to use the information to heal, grow, and move toward love and inner peace.

The objective of this exercise is to understand that (1) the Level of Consciousness, in the context of the Integrated Self Model, is a measure of personal energetic vibration that we experience, depending on where our personal state of emotion resides, on average, (2) our emotions have identifiable vibrations, which correlate to our personal level of consciousness, and (3) to use this understanding to effectively manage our personal emotions, our energetic vibration, and, ultimately, our level of consciousness,

> In describing the emotional correlates of the energy fields of consciousness, keep in mind that they're rarely manifested as pure states in an individual. Levels of consciousness are always mixed; a person may operate on one level in a given area of life and on quite another level in another area. An individual's overall level of consciousness is the sum total effect of these various levels.[50]
>
> As we look at the Map of Consciousness, it becomes clear that the calibrated levels correlate with specific processes of consciousness—emotions, perceptions, or attributes, worldviews and spiritual beliefs.[51]

Following is the Map of Consciousness[52] from Hawkins' book.

MAP OF CONSCIOUSNESS (Power vs. Force, David R. Hawkins, 2002)					
God-View	Self-View	Level	Log	Emotion	Process
Self	Is	Enlightenment	700 - 1,000	Ineffable	Pure Consciousness
All-Being	Perfect	Peace	600	Bliss	Illumination
One	Complete	Joy	540	Serenity	Transfiguration
Loving	Benign	Love	500	Reverence	Revelation
Wise	Meaningful	Reason	400	Understanding	Abstraction
Merciful	Harmonious	Acceptance	350	Forgiveness	Transcendence
Inspiring	Hopeful	Willingness	310	Optimism	Intention
Enabling	Satisfactory	Neutrality	250	Trust	Release
Permitting	Feasible	Courage	200	Affirmation	Empowerment
Indifferent	Demanding	Pride	175	Scorn	Inflation
Vengeful	Antagonistic	Anger	150	Hate	Aggression
Denying	Disappointing	Desire	125	Craving	Enslavement
Punitive	Frightening	Fear	100	Anxiety	Withdrawal
Uncaring	Tragic	Grief	75	Regret	Despondency
Condemning	Hopeless	Apathy	50	Despair	Abdication
Vindictive	Evil	Guilt	30	Blame	Destruction
Despising	Hateful	Shame	20	Humiliation	Elimination

Short Descriptions of the Levels of Human Consciousness, excerpts from Hawkins:[53]

- Energy Level 20: Shame—This level is perilously proximate (close) to death.
- Energy Level 30: Guilt—Guilt is commonly used to manipulate and punish.
- Energy Level 50: Apathy—Characterized by poverty, despair, and hopelessness.
- Energy Level 75: Grief—This is the level of sadness, loss, and dependency.
- Energy Level 100: Fear—Limits the growth of the personality and leads to inhibition.
- Energy Level 125: Desire—Motivates vast areas of human activity; Also addiction.
- Energy Level 150: Anger—This can lead to either constructive or destructive action.
- Energy Level 175: Pride—People feel positive when they reach this level in contrast.
- Energy Level 200: Courage—Power first appears here; a line for positive/negative.
- Energy Level 250: Neutrality—Energy becomes very positive at this level and above.
- Energy Level 310: Willingness—Rapid growth; has overcome inner resistance to life.
- Energy Level 350: Acceptance—Understands one is source/creator of life experience.
- Energy Level 400: Reason—Intelligence and rationality; knowledge and education.
- Energy Level 500: Love—Unconditional, unchanging, permanent; a state of being.
- Energy Level 540: Joy—Love as inner Joy; from within each moment of existence.
- Energy Level 600: Peace—Bliss; transcendence, self-realization, God-consciousness.

The Steps to Work on Self Growth and Advance Your Level of Consciousness

Now that you have this basic understanding of the levels of Consciousness, it is useful for you to know how to use this information, along with your efforts to create balance between your Ego and your Soul, to improve your level of Consciousness and the quality of your life. Consider the following steps to help you assess (1) where you are on the scale of Consciousness, (2) where you want to be, and (3) the aligned actions needed to reach your goal:

1. Familiarize yourself with the "Level" name and the associated "Emotion."
2. Take some time to reflect on the emotion or emotions which comprise your average days in your normal week.
3. Once you have identified the typical set of emotions that you experience during a normal day or week, estimate how much (as a percentage) of that period of time you are experiencing that emotion.
4. Next, notice the Level/Emotion with the highest percentage. This is your normal, average, or median level of Consciousness (depending on how high the percentage is compared to the other Levels/Emotions on your list).
5. Next, notice the Level/Emotion that you have indicated which resides at the lower levels on the scale of Consciousness. This may be the Emotion for you to work on first, depending on the percentage of your day experiencing that Emotion.
6. Next, build a personal development plan to reduce the percentage of time that you are in that Emotion, and the negative impact this Emotion is having on your day-to-day life. (Note: This step will be rather subjective, that is, understanding how much it impacts you and your life is intimately personal and will influence your plan.)
7. Determine the level of support that will be required to address the specific issues identified and the level of per-

sonal impact. For example, the level of support required will depend on whether the identified issue is trauma, anxiety, depression, anger, fitness, weight, diet, relationship, parenting, career, etc. You may need to engage a skilled professional, such as a therapist, life coach, holistic health practitioner, personal trainer, etc., or maybe you only need an accountability partner. (Note: For trauma work, be sure to engage a professional who specifically is trauma trained.)

8. Record your baseline of Levels/Emotions/percentage, and assign a level of impact to each, using the Solution-Focused method of assigning a number from 1 to 100, where 1 is the least desirable situation, and 100 is the most desirable. The objective is to track your progress, either up or down, and eventually see a steady improvement over time in response to the specific actions that you are taking.
9. Maintain a record of your baseline and your progress, assessing where you are, at least once per week. Make note of significant changes and causes for these changes.
10. Allow enough time during (and immediately following) your significant growth periods for the healing, improvements, and positive changes to be integrated into your Self; that is, allow time for the new you to become a part of your personal identity.
11. Update your personal development plan and specific aligned actions as appropriate.

While I feel strongly about the importance of understanding the levels of consciousness, how they relate to your energy, to your vibration, and to your life, and also how to best apply this knowledge to have the most positive impact on your day-to-day life, I want to caution you. The steps of assessing the levels of consciousness for yourself are not intended to be a way for you to compare yourself to others. Typically, you would not share your own level of consciousness or even know the level of consciousness of others. Comparison and judgment are elements of ego and can be associated with the energy levels of pride and desire.

The level of consciousness for me is a way for me to monitor my own level of vibration and to assess relatively where I am now and where I want to be in the future. If my current goal in life is to live in a consistent state of peace (with only occasional dips when triggered), I will set my sights on level 500, that being the level of Love on the scale of consciousness. Once I have identified where my average day is currently on the scale, I will make a plan, set some goals, and begin to make incremental changes in my thoughts and behaviors that will help me increase my level of vibration, with a personal goal of moving up one level at a time.

If you want to get to the highest level of vibration in this lifetime, then you will want to set a personal goal to move toward living in a state of love, living a life of authenticity, and continuing to expand your level of consciousness through personal and spiritual practices that support living a life of love. As you incrementally increase your personal vibration and level of consciousness, be sure to allow time at the different levels of consciousness for this new way of being in the world to become integrated into your Self identity, or you may notice that you have periods of time when you feel like you are taking a step or two in a backward direction. Once you have reached the consistent vibrational state of love, continue living life authentically as you advance toward a higher level of vibration and consciousness, elevating your energy and vibration to that of joy, and then eventually the level of Peace.

Remember, there is no one level of consciousness better than another level. There is value and opportunity for growth at every level. However, if you feel inspired to expand your level of consciousness, I encourage you to go back through this part of the book, assess where you are on the scale of consciousness, identify where you would like to be, and then establish a plan to get you from where you are today to where you want to go. The choice is yours, and yours alone.

Section 5.9—Assess Personal Ego Identity

As we have already discussed, the two most powerful questions that will drive us toward personal Ego growth and toward a higher version of ourselves are: "Who am I?" and "Who do I want to be?" Once you have answered these two questions, the next question will be, "How do I get there from where I am today?"

Let's explore these questions using my experience as an example of what you may want to consider when working to identify your answers. Remember that each of us is on our own unique path and having our own human-spirit experience. Meet yourself wherever you are without judgment or criticism in the spirit and practice of self-love.

Who am I?

As I shared in the section on my personal development, the single most supportive and informational personal development tool for me was the Myers-Briggs Type Indicator (MBTI) test. The results hit deeply, and it was the catalyst for my Ego becoming aware of itself. More precisely, it was the moment that my conscious mind became aware of my subconscious mind, and the out-of-balance impact that the subconscious mind had on my actions and reactions in all aspects of my life.

To answer the profound question of, "Who am I?" we need to obtain an unbiased, and somewhat more objective view of our human personality traits. It is not advisable to ask those friends and family members who are close to us for this input, as their answers will be based on their lens of perception of you. Criticism, whether intended to be constructive or otherwise, tends to sting and bruise the Ego, even for those of us with a solid, well-developed self-image. Even though the results of the MBTI test may seem to be quite accurate for each of us as an individual, we need to remember that it is not targeting us personally. The MBTI test is only a tool that provides information to us, and it is only you as a human that assigns a personal meaning to this information. Pay attention to any feelings or emotional reactions that reveal themselves in the process. It will be essential for us to identify any feelings related to these discoveries in order for us to effectively attend to and heal the inner child wounds at some later point in this process.

The MBTI test was administered to me by an authorized practitioner for the IT department in my workplace thirty years ago. Overall, there are sixteen Myers-Briggs personality types, that is, sixteen different groupings of four pairs of type preferences. (This will become more clear as you continue to read.) Each of these personality types has an identified collection of personality characteristics and traits that are typical for those people who have tested to be most aligned with each one of the sixteen particular personality types. Please note that the more precise MBTI test administered by a trained practitioner will provide scores with a range for each pair of preferences, which means that you may at times act according to one set of traits in some situations and then according to the other set of traits in other situations.

The four pairs of Myers-Briggs Type Preferences are: Extraversion (E)—Introversion (I), Intuition (N)—Sensing (S), Thinking (T)—Feeling (F), and (4) Judging (J)—Perceiving (P). The sixteen specific types consist of combinations of these four pairs. For more information regarding MBTI, check out my favorite reference books, *Please Understand Me*[54] and *Gifts Differing*.[55]

My Myers-Briggs personality type indicator at the time I was tested came out to be a very strong and consistent ISTJ, which stands for introversion, sensing, thinking, and judging. According to "Please Understand Me,"

> ISTJs are characterized by decisiveness in practical affairs... dependable would best describe this type... The word of ISTJs is their bond... Whether at home or at work, this type is rather quiet and serious. ISTJs are extraordinarily persevering and dependable... They perform their duties without flourish or fanfare [and their] dedication can go unnoticed and unappreciated... Interested in thoroughness, details, justice, practical procedures, and smooth flow of personnel and material... ISTJs can handle difficult, detailed figures and make sense of them.

> They communicate a message of reliability and stability... ISTJs are patient with their work and with procedures within an institution, although not always patient with the individual goals of people...[56] and much, much more!

Who do I want to be?

Once I held the results of the MBTI in my hands, I dug into the available references to understand the results in great detail and interpret what the results meant for me specifically. During my reading, I noticed that the descriptions and explanations related to the ISTJ seemed to be extremely on point for me. Most of the characteristics and traits noted were accepted by me as being very positive traits (in my opinion, anyway). I felt very proud of being someone who was being described as detail-oriented, dependable, and capable.

However, there was one aspect in particular that hit me hard. My studying and understanding of the MBTI resources revealed to me that people with my personality type will typically minimize and even ignore the feelings of other people while getting the job done as planned and according to procedures. I reflected on this information and quickly realized that I was being a "jerk" to people, and that was in fact true. I decided in that moment that I would work on improving my communication and relationships with people.

Now that I had information and insight from the Myers-Briggs Type Indicator Test regarding who I am, and subsequently, who I wanted to become, my next step was to create an inventory of the personality traits that I perceived to be my strengths, along with a list of traits that provide room for growth. I would encourage you to do the same for yourself. Below you will find my list of strengths and areas for growth and improvement.

Strengths: Determination, hard worker, clear thinker, sense of integrity, knows right from wrong, strength of convictions, attention to detail, compassionate, giving

Areas for growth: patience, emotional connection to others, tendency to isolate, critical, reactive to criticism

How do I get there from where I am today?

Now that I decided with commitment and conviction that I would work hard on improving my communications and relationships with people, I now needed to take aligned action toward these goals. Over the next fifteen years or so after this decision, I (1) read several books on interpersonal communication and relationships, (2) earned a bachelor's degree in communication, and (3) earned a master's degree in counseling psychology and counselor education. During the same time period, I was also committed to and working toward my spiritual development and Soul evolution.

After the personal development and growth occurred in the area of relating better toward people, I still test out as an ISTJ personality type when the test is specifically related to my IT professional work as a certified Project Manager. However, the MBTI test now identifies me as an INFJ personality type when the focus of the test is on people and relationships. According to the referenced books,

> INFJs have an unusually strong drive to contribute to the welfare of others and genuinely enjoy helping their fellow men. INFJs make outstanding individual therapists who have the ability to get in touch with the archetypes of their patients. At work as well as socially, INFJs are highly sensitive in their handling of others and tend to work well in organizational structure.[57]

I then was able to achieve balance at work between the project goals and the relationships with the people involved.

According to Life Coach Adri Thomas,

> Something I think is really cool about growing and changing and developing into this human is that we can change core beliefs that we have about ourselves. We first need to figure out what those core beliefs are, but just because

> we have thought something or something was ingrained in us since childhood doesn't mean that that's an identity that we still need to live by… I know as a life coach and as somebody who has survived a very toxic family what it is like to have to now rewire my brain to not think certain things about myself. If you want to change your core belief about yourself, the first thing you need to do is recognize the core beliefs that you have about yourself. The second thing you need to do is [consider]…what do I want to fully believe about myself. And the third thing you need to do is…ask yourself if I believe this about myself…how would my life be different, what would it look like. It is 100 percent possible to heal from these core beliefs and, just because something feels familiar doesn't mean it's always going to feel accurate to you. You have the ability to rewire your mind.[58]

Building on this approach of changing our core beliefs of who we are, Transformational Mindset Coach Tiffany Gingrich says, now that…

> you know it's you…you're the one who's been getting in your own way with these patterns you've just been recreating your entire life. When we're not aware of exactly what's going on in our subconscious minds, then we're just living life by default…just with whatever was programmed in when we were kids, but there is a better way. You can create conscious awareness around your patterns, around your thoughts, your behaviors, and the emotions that you're experiencing from day to day. And it all begins with awareness around the identity that you've had about yourself and if

> it's serving you or not, and an awareness around the stories that you continue to tell yourself. And once you are aware of exactly what these patterns of self sabotage are that are living in the subconscious mind, then we [can] begin to introduce subconscious reprogramming, and the way that we do that is through repetition. This can be done through meditation, hypnosis, or affirmations... That is how we reprogram the subconscious mind.[59]

Once you get to this point of your awareness of Self, once you have gained an understanding of the current state of your Ego development and your Soul evolution, of where you are, and of where you want to be, I recommend that you engage with a skilled professional such as a therapist, life coach, wellness coach, or holistic health practitioner (depending on your individual goals) to create a personal development plan for how to get to where you want to go from exactly where you are today. You can always choose to walk this path of self-examination, healing, and growth by yourself. However, it may take longer because your Ego will struggle to keep you unchanged and safe in your comfort zone. Whatever you have been doing so far in life, whether consciously or unconsciously, has kept you alive. By working with a professional in the area of growth you are looking for, you have support, insight, and accountability to make consistent progress along your journey through the resistance and the unlearning of subconscious programming.

In the end, the course of our human-spirit experience and whether we effectively use this precious lifetime for personal growth, spiritual evolution, and expanding consciousness comes down to *choice*. In the Integrated Self Model, we hold out *choice* as the single most consequential determinant on our conscious path to your authentic Self and inner peace. Sure, when we are faced with making a choice, difficult or otherwise, we are usually acting or reacting to human intervention, divine intervention, or divine inspiration. However, it is the consistency of the choices, and the level of commitment to each choice, that serves to propel us along the human-spirit journey at different speeds, and with varying results. Are you choosing consciously or unconsciously?

Spiritual leader Deepak Chopra emphasizes the huge role and influence that choice has in our lifetime and how to best operate within the spiritual Law of Karma,

> You and I are essentially infinite choice-makers. In every moment of our existence, we are in that field of all possibilities where we have access to an infinity of choices. Some of these choices are made consciously, while others are made unconsciously. But the best way to understand and maximize the use of karmic law is to become consciously aware of the choices we make in every moment… When you make any choice—any choice at all—you can ask yourself two things: First of all, 'What are the consequences of this choice that I am making?' In your heart you will immediately know what these are. Secondly, 'Will this choice that I am making now bring happiness to me and to those around me?' If the answer is yes, then go ahead with that choice. If the answer is no, if that choice brings distress either to you or to those around you, then don't make that choice. It's as simple as that.[60]

Transformational Mindset Coach, Tiffany Gingrich emphasizes the importance that choice plays in our lives, and that it is on us to choose wisely.

> Everything is really a choice; how we feel, how we think, how we behave, who we show up as. But you can really kind of boil it down to two choices we can make. (1) We could take the path we've always taken; we can do things the

> way we've always done them. You know, the way we were taught prior to age seven by God knows who…and whatever beliefs that they had were put into our mind; we didn't even get a choice. So we could go by their standards and their thinking and just live our entire life unconsciously, making choices dependent on keeping us safe, never trying anything too new, never stepping into the unknown, and doing your habits the same every day, talking about yourself in the same negative ways. Just taking the path of least resistance; it's safe…even if you're miserable, it's predictable. Or we take the second path in life, which is the unknown, which is really scary, I know. And the growth zone, that's where freedom is. That's where true confidence comes from. That's when we get to choose what we believe. We get to choose what we want to change about ourselves. So if you found yourself unconsciously walking down that same old path you've been going down your whole life…but you sense that you're meant for more, that you're here to do more. That's your higher Self calling. It's saying, 'get over here in the growth zone, so we can live a happier, healthier, more exciting life.' And so my question to you [today] is: Which do you choose?[61]

Life and Mindset Coach, Melissa Nicole further emphasizes the importance of choice and consciously choosing.

> When we see life for what it is, and not what it should be, what we're doing is removing the expectations that we have on people, and on situations. And when we see it for what it is, life is a lot easier; it's more peaceful. We stop taking things so personally. We go with the flow. We

> let things be. We accept things for: as they are. And then what we start doing is we're letting go of what happened in the past; we let go of what was. Our past does not define us. All the past is doing is giving us lessons so we can grow, so we can learn, so we can evolve. And we can apply it to our present day, so we can accept things for: as they are. So accept what is. Let go of what was. And start having faith in what will be. The simple mindset is actually so freeing. Holding on to something, what should have been, could have been, would have been...all it's doing is holding you back from your full potential. Accept. Let go. Have faith. Choose Yourself...and Choose Love.[62]

Now that you have examined your personal history, identified what has inspired and motivated you to bravely push through life's circumstances, pinpointed your personal struggles and obstacles that have held you back, and understand yourself deeper, you now have a chance, a choice, to choose a new path and rewrite your past to change the trajectory of your future timeline. So what will you choose?

Section 5.10—Reframe and Rewrite Your Personal Story

At this point of the exercise, we should now have a very good understanding of the story that we have personalized and anchored into during our childhood years; the very personal story to which we added chapter after chapter from our own biased perspective and interpretation as we advanced through young adulthood to where we are today. We should also now have at least a basic understanding of the personal identity that we initially formed, tested, and modified during our teenage years and continued to hone and perfect through the daily struggles of adult life, supported by the formation of adaptive skills and enhanced by personal growth from opportunities of choice during our adult years.

Now that we have experienced life in real ways with a measure of maturity that we could not possibly have as a child growing up, we can now look at the original story from a new perspective and consider a new level of understanding and truth. We can now consider the key time periods of our lives and how the story can be appropriately reframed in a more holistic and balanced view. Note that this first effort to reframe your story is not about ignoring the facts of what actually occurred, nor is it about practicing toxic positivity which tends to invalidate the human experience. The idea of this first pass is to rewrite our story with tempered emotions, where we can look at the story holistically from not only our vulnerable, childlike perspective but also from the perspectives of others. To be clear, it is not our intention when rewriting our story to ignore childhood experiences or sugarcoat situations such as trauma or abuse to create an imagined happy ending. Another factor in how you rewrite your story will be the level to which you have worked on and processed your childhood experiences, including any trauma or inner child wounds.

Reframe and rewrite your story from wherever you are right now; be honest and real. Do not adjust your story based on how you think you should be feeling now as an adult, but modify your original story only to the extent that is authentic to you at the moment. You will have the opportunity to reframe and rewrite your story at various points throughout your lifetime as you mature, grow, and heal. Even though our stories change constantly, it is only really useful to do this exercise at significant milestones in your life. In retrospect, I find that I have only consciously considered my life story at perhaps three different points in time. Let's walk through this exercise and continue using my story and experience as an example of how to approach this.

Recap of my original story: This original story is from the perspective of a thirty-five-year-old person who only knew a life of dealing with childhood issues as a constructed adult persona (previously mentioned, but summarized here to help you through this exercise).

I grew up in a home with parents who were not nurturing or attentive, and who were emotionally neglectful to myself and my siblings. There was very little attention given to me by my core family and I felt as if I were invisible, devalued, and unloved. However, extended family members did provide nurturing, attention, and love to me that served to supplement what I was not getting in the core family home. There was no abuse evident in the family, especially not in my house. My mother stayed home all of the time, so I felt safe and secure. We did not have a lot of money, but we never went hungry. My childhood experience caused me to develop the following personality traits: hypervigilance, people-pleasing tendencies, perfectionism, introversion, limiting beliefs around money, and lack of validation from my father. In order to survive and thrive in the adult world, at the age of twelve I developed a persona of being confident, capable, and outgoing which carried me as I moved forward in life in spite of my ingrained fears.

Rewrite of my original story 1: When I was about thirty-five years old, I started to come out of a sleepwalking state. I became aware that my subconscious mind had been directly influencing my conscious thoughts, actions, and reactions. At the same moment, I also became aware of a spiritual consciousness that quickly took on the role of a discerning observer, watching my thoughts and actions like a trusted advisor. It was not until almost twenty years later that I reached a significant milestone, a point of emotional and spiritual stability when I would reassess my childhood experiences and rewrite my life story from a new perspective of compassion and understanding. I was able to reach this new point of clarity and discernment only after my extensive personal growth work to address my childhood issues, heal my inner child wounds, experience a spiritual awakening, and education in counseling psychology. Here is the new rewrite of my original story with a new perspective:

I grew up in a home with parents who were not able to be nurturing or attentive to the children. Each of my parents grew up in homes with parents who were not nurturing either, and who were dramatically influenced by the Great Depression of 1929, in addition to the harsh reality that followed. My father's father died when my father was thirteen years old, which surely impacted my father as a parent.

As a result of my parents' individual upbringing, they were emotionally neglectful to me and my siblings. While this lack of empathy and nurturing by my parents may not have been intentional or their fault, the results were the same as in my original story. There was very little attention given to me by my parents, and I felt as if I were invisible and not loved. I now realize that I was loved, though not in the ways that would be understood by me until I was older. My extended family members provided love, support, and attention to supplement what I was not getting from my parents so I was able to move ahead with my life. My mother staying home provided a sense of safety and security. We did not have a lot of money, but we never went hungry. I developed personality traits such as hypervigilance, perfectionism, people-pleasing, introversion, and a thirst for validation. I came to develop a persona of a confident, capable, and outgoing individual who moved forward in life despite the fears carried by my inner child.

I now understand that this constructed persona that I created when I was twelve years old to keep my inner child safe while I moved through the real world was actually my real Self, my authentic Self. This persona was truly who I was before all of the childhood experiences and subconscious programming occurred. It was now up to my authentic Self to keep my inner child safe from the noisy, external world. It was up to my authentic Self to allow "us" to be seen in the world, be validated, and be loved.

*****

As you can see, the new overall story and my childhood issues did not change much from the original. However, what did change was the meaning of my parents' emotional neglect. My parents did not consciously or intentionally neglect their children's emotions and mental health. Unfortunately, they were not equipped with the tools and emotional maturity to raise mentally healthy children. My parents were not really at fault, at least no more at fault than the lineage of ancestors that came before them. This makes it easier for me to forgive them and forgive the situation that I was born into. In this version of my story, while they are not blamed for my childhood experiences and resulting wounds, they also get no credit for the healing and growth that occurred later in life. To be fair, however, they do get credit for providing basic needs.

Rewrite of my original story 2: Today in my current state of self-perceived emotional and spiritual consciousness, the story of my life would be much different. I can honestly say that I am eternally grateful for each and every one of the human-spirit experiences that provided the opportunities for me to make choices to become this truly conscious version of myself that I am today. I understand that this may be a controversial statement to those who are currently in or have survived an abusive or traumatic situation. I understand that my experiences are not the same and I am not suggesting that they should feel thankful for those experiences. I just know that I was extremely angry at God at several points in my journey and I told Him so. Being on the other side of the pain and with my expanded consciousness, I can sincerely say that I love who I am, who I have become, and who I always was.

The ultimate rewrite of my life story would be a direct reflection of my spiritual beliefs, which now extend outside of this physical world. My story would have all of the elements of spirituality that I now hold dear to me, even those elements that may lie outside the spiritual beliefs of others. I can go on about my spiritual beliefs, providing explanations and details of my personal belief system, but why would that matter to anyone else? This is where your own spiritual belief system comes in, and where your own story matters.

Your own personal spiritual belief system is the only one that should truly matter to you. It might morph and evolve as you go through different seasons of your life. What is your spiritual belief system? What are your beliefs around the existence of God, Source, Spirit, the Creator (whatever words you connect with) that you hold onto today? It is very important that you understand your spiritual beliefs and that you question them at some point. In this way, your beliefs will either grow stronger, or you will modify your beliefs to support whoever you are at that moment and who you want to become.

Section 5.11—Achieving Balance and Integration

The Integrated Self Model is all about creating balance by integrating the pieces of your humanness (Ego development) and your divinity (Soul evolution) to fully embody your integrated Self. The model maps out the integration of the development of the Ego and the evolution of the Soul together from which you can maximize your human-spirit potential and move through the real world in flow. The Integrated Self Model will support both your personal and spiritual growth until you get to a defining point where you have finally created balance between the two sides when you no longer have to focus on one side or the other to regain balance. You can then consciously stay in balance as you grow, both personally and spiritually to actualize a life of harmony and prosperity. Through self-awareness, you are able to maintain balance, organically.

One of the skills related to the integration of the Ego and the Soul is managing the Ego and modifying behavior. I have become proficient at modifying the thoughts that drive my behavior and then working with my ego, subconscious, and inner child to get different outcomes. One thing I want to be clear about is that the Integrated Self Model is all about lovingly embracing the Ego and developing a mutual trust and partnership with the Soul. We are not advocating for the destruction of the Ego, as the term "ego death" is popular among those who aim to reject our innate humanness and work hard to only embrace the spiritual aspect of their human-spirit experience. You will not be able to advance very far spiritually if you have not engaged your Ego in partnership with your Soul, and if you are not actively and consciously working toward balanced personal and spiritual growth.

One critical and essential factor that allowed me to, and continues to allow me to make clear unbiased assessments, fair ethical decisions, and take quick action was the ultimate source of my inner voice and inner dialogue. Since I had essentially grown up alone, separate from the rest of the family, and explored the world by myself, I felt invisible and very alone in life. With the lack of conversation growing up, you'd think that this would set me up for a lifetime of challenges and depression; however, this was literally a blessing in disguise. Without the voices and opinions of everyone else in my ears, I only had my own voice to listen to.

As a young child, I was curious and adventurous, trying things out, making mistakes, and then fixing them. I wasn't taught that making mistakes was silly or bad, in fact, I grew up knowing that making mistakes was a natural and normal part of the problem-solving process in life, "If at first, you don't succeed, try and try again," was one mantra I lived by. Instead of learning that making mistakes is wrong, I learned that other people were trouble and that I only had myself to rely on. I learned that it was best to stay away from other people, and because of that, I didn't have other voices in my head. Today, I am able to make clear distinctions between the voices in my head whether it be my Ego and subconscious, or my Soul and higher Self. By integrating new thoughts, behaviors, and actions that align with my integrated Self, consciousness expands and allows for new possibilities and experiences.

Neville Goddard describes the importance of recognizing and understanding the existence of consciousness,

> It is of vital importance to understand clearly just what consciousness is. The reason lies in the fact that consciousness is the one and only reality; it is the first and only cause-substance of the phenomena of life. Nothing has existence for man [except] through the consciousness that he has of it… It is the only foundation on which the phenomena of life can be explained.[63]

I learned that trying new things, making mistakes, and then choosing to learn from those mistakes (or not) was being human, perfectly human. Just as I somehow knew that my God was not an angry, vengeful, punitive God as the church tried to teach me, I also somehow came to know early in life that I was perfect. I know we're all familiar with the saying that "humans are perfectly imperfect," and how that implies that as humans we're full of imperfections that keep the Ego engaged, in control, and validated. What if we instead changed this phrase to be that we are "perfectly human" or perfect period. I have come to know that we are perfect because God does not make mistakes. Once we start considering that we may be just perfect, we begin to chip away at the harmful stories that others have told us, that we have told ourselves, that say we are bad, damaged, broken, unlovable, and unwanted. We must reframe our experiences and rewrite our stories. We must begin to experience our lives consciously, and with kindness, compassion, and love for ourselves.

As explained by The Inner Child Whisperer, Stephanie Saint Claire,

> The healing journey is actually a terrible term for this experience of finding ourselves, because a journey implies that I have to leave myself, to find myself. It also implies that there is a self to find. We can incorrectly believe that we have a "perfect" Self to find, that has all the attributes that we consider "good" and "enlightened" and "right." But this idealized self is just another ego-based personality, just another creation. It's like a set of clothing that you learn to put on to be acceptable to the egos of the people around you…and over time you start believing that the clothes ARE you. And the problem here is obvious: as soon as "the clothes" get dirty or snagged or shabby, or go out of fashion, or start to make you walk funny because they fit too tight, you think that YOU are the problem, because you're identified with your "clothes." But you could never be a problem. You could never be anything but perfect. You are perfect right now exactly as you are. You don't have to do more work. You don't need

> to learn how to meditate better. You don't need to do yoga every day or take silent retreats. You don't need to learn astrology, or go to church, or pray. You don't need to do anything... and you don't need to go anywhere to be healed. There's nothing to heal from, except that belief that 1.) you are your personality...you are your 'clothes', and 2.) your quirks, 'issues' and 'flaws' are mistakes to be ashamed of, as opposed to adaptations to be retired. And none of this requires that you 'work harder'; this doesn't require a lot of effort. You get to wake up, and it can literally take one second of awareness. You're perfect exactly as you are.[64]

Saint Claire goes on to say,

> Life only wants to be loved by you. Life wants you to love it, just as much as life loves you. Our job, our only job, in this life, is to remove all of the delusions and obstacles to being in joy... and that means that you've got to wake up from the beliefs you have that there's anything wrong with you... that you're broken, or flawed, or need to be fixed. Because it's all [nonsense]. You are a spirit having a human experience, and all of the things that you think are wrong about you, those were all ways that you picked up that helped you survive a gnarly childhood. That's it. It's just that you've come to believe that those survival adaptations are who you are... and they're not. They're like clothes; they're really sticky clothes, but they're clothes... and you can take them off... because life is waiting for you to love it. Don't wait.[65]

If your goal is to feel content, peaceful, and empowered in your everyday life and not just in the moments that you find yourself alone, separated, and safe from the rest of the world, then you must remember that you have both an Ego and a Soul and that each plays a significant role in your human-spirit experience. While it may be counter-intuitive and go against some teachings in the broad landscape of the spiritual community, you must pay attention to your Ego instead of discarding it from the full picture. If you work on developing your spiritual practices and growing your consciousness without taking care of your Ego alongside your Soul, you are not going to evolve very far toward peace; in fact, you may experience anxiety, stress, drama, and confusion from the imbalance of consciousness and evolution.

Eckhardt Tolle talks about the effects of the ego, "As long as the egoic mind is running your life, you cannot truly be at ease; you cannot be at peace or fulfilled except for brief intervals when you obtained what you wanted when a craving has just been fulfilled."[66]

This balance that you strive to maintain is between your spirituality and the practical world. It is maintained by making sure that the Ego is not left behind, and that the whispers of your Soul are not neglected. If you neglect one or the other, it can bring about resistance in the form of stress, confusion, anxiety, or depression. If you are missing either the Ego or the Soul, you will not experience wholeness or feeling complete. Integration of both the Ego and Soul is what we call the Integrated Self. We do not just have one aspect of Self, and these two parts are not meant to be side by side, but integrated into the whole to be congruent, acting like you believe and believing like you act.

Once you get these two parts of Self congruent and balanced, your level of consciousness will expand. Even if you haven't completely integrated both aspects, you are going to see significant growth. When you get to a level of consciousness above the level of 200 (which is the level of integrity according to the book *Power vs. Force* by David Hawkins) and are able to maintain that level of integrity, things will start building and building. This doesn't mean that you never experience any lower vibrational emotions, but rather you use them as indicators of what might be needing your attention at that time. There is value in these lower frequencies that we experience, and if you feel stuck in these frequencies of shame, guilt, or despair, ask for help and grab someone's hand. There is no shame in asking for help, even though it may feel that way to you.

We are not hiding anymore from who we were always meant to be. If you do not believe that you were born with an earthly purpose, then who do you want to be? Who do you envision when you imagine a future version of yourself that is fulfilled and at peace? That version of you already exists; there might just be a disconnection caused by your life experience and subconscious programming. The human-spirit experience can be enjoyable if we learn to live in flow and release our resistance to it, as nothing has meaning besides the meaning we assign to things through our current perspective and level of consciousness. Once you get to the other side of the pain, life will feel amazing. You still experience the ups and downs, but once you know that you are whole, aware, seen, loved, and valued by yourself, life gets to be peaceful and liberating.

Transformational Mindset Coach, Tiffany Gingrich reminds us to celebrate where we are right now and how far we have come and offers some techniques for achieving personal freedom and growth,

> Stop and notice how far you came…all of the goals that you have already reached. And if you haven't been reaching them and you've been stuck, that's okay too; it's a part of the journey. Let me tell you what's absolutely scientifically proven and works in our lives… (1) Meditation: It completely changes the brain. (2) Subconscious reprogramming: It completely changes the script going on in the brain, the belief system, so that you begin to believe in yourself and in your abilities…and that you already have all of the resources within that you can tap into…and that creates infinite potential in your life. (3) Looking at your daily habits: Are they serving you? Are they get-

> ting you to where you want to go in life? Or do they kind of suck? (4) Dopamine: Are you heavily addicted to dopamine…and in your phone all day long scrolling, losing hours of your life to the dopamine roller coaster called screen time? (5) Paying attention to the languaging going on inside your mind and what you're saying about yourself and your circumstances every day. (6) Spirituality: Anything that fills your soul back up and replenishes you. And finally… It would be having accountability in your life; someone to hold you accountable for what you said you want to create more, because alone we revert to our old brain patterns and together we are stronger, and we can get to where we're going to go together. So just a little reminder today to celebrate your win, celebrate how far you've come, and never ever give up…because it only gets better. Trust me.[67]

Once you become aware of the roles that your conscious and subconscious minds play in forming your personal identity and how your identity influences your choices, you can become the observer through consciousness and begin to make choices that are more aligned with your authentic Self. You will come to experience more contentment and peace in your life through aligned choices. Once you become spiritually awakened and evolve to the point where you are able to embrace your ego as an essential part of the holistic Self, you will be able to move consciously toward balance, integration, and peace. My wish for you is that you wake up today, you become aware there's a better way to live life. You will be amazed by how good life can be once you are able to bring your Ego and your Soul into balance, expand your consciousness, and move along the path toward inner peace.

PART 6

The End of our Journey and the Beginning of Yours

Section 6.1—Now That You Know, What Are You Going to Do?

Now that you know your story, who you really are, how your experiences made you into who you are today, that there is nothing wrong with you, and that you are exactly where you are supposed to be, what are you going to do with this knowledge? What do you want to create from the power that you now know lies within each and every one of us? Are you ready to take the next step toward becoming the best version of your Self?

When we become aware of our Ego, when our Soul awakens and begins to evolve, when growth is realized in a conscious, balanced manner, the next natural questions that arise organically are: Why am I here? What is my purpose? A lot of people assume that your *purpose* is directly tied to your career or job. We want to emphasize that this isn't always the case. Our purposes do not have to be something we consciously do, work on, and provide for people. Maybe your purpose is to break the patterns that have kept your lineage stuck in a victim mindset, maybe your purpose is to provide a nurturing home for your children or maybe your purpose is to just be a light in this world that affects everyone you meet, maybe your purpose is to educate people on something you're passionate about and create a community.

Once we accept that we are all here for a reason, we can come to understand that everyone's purposes matter equally and that everyone's purpose will be at different magnitudes, but not a hierarchy. Perhaps from the inspirations of this book you now know that the answers to all of your questions already lie within and are accessible to you. All you need to do is seek and you shall find the answers to whatever you need to know. Keep in mind that you may receive your answer through a new idea or thought, a feeling, a sign in your reality, or an inner knowing. Self-awareness is your best friend when it comes to following your heart and reprogramming the mind.

The more that you're able to flow through adversity by staying centered and grounded, the more that you can be in the present moment and live from your heart center, the easier information and inspiration will flow through you exactly when you need it,

> When you have the ability to stand your ground on this third dimensional plane and [know] what your sole purpose is, what you are passionate about doing in this lifetime as a soul, you can then connect up to God's source and ask for all the help from that infinite intelligence. The more that you practice this presence and solidify your mark here by doing exactly what you need to do to make this happen, you're going to notice your life explode; there are going to be so many miracles.[68]
>
> When you start your spiritual journey, you'll be shown just how far you are from your authenticity, just how much you need and want to change. Purging everything that is unaligned is not an easy process. You may or may not be prepared for the removal of distractions, bad habits, people who hold you back. It does, however, give you the backbone that you need to create the life that is aligned with you. It shows you that

> you are all that you need to make it happen. Your whole life will be deconstructed into the most beautiful, fulfilling life you could ever imagine. Proceed with caution and excitement.[69]

Regardless of whether you already know your purpose down to your Soul, or whether you have no clue as to what your purpose is or how to go about figuring it out, you now have a choice. You are now aware of the role that your Ego and subconscious mind have played up to this point in your life journey. Whether you are feeling stuck in the moment, you are doing alright, or you are just ready to take the next step toward becoming the next best version of yourself, it all comes down to one choice, that is, the next choice. You will need to do the work with intention and connection, connecting to your inner Self and who you are at your core being, at your Soul level.

> Connecting to who you really are is being okay with anything that comes your way from the outside. You realize what matters is being aligned with yourself. Learning to let things just be, so this way more exciting experiences can come your way and this will happen... Your mind will be clear and more focused on what you really want, and who you really want to be... You will love where you are in the present moment in your life, when you know you've changed. You will be grateful for what is. Once we practice the techniques of meditation, awareness of our thoughts, letting go of the past and stopping those thoughts about the future, you will start to shed layers of yourself and become the real you. You are changing your brain patterns and the years of conditioning. You are combining the logic and creative side of your brain. It takes time to rewire your brain. You will soon notice that you are changing. Things around you will not

affect you like they used to. You will not react to situations like you may have in the past. You start to live in the moment… Trust the process! When you start to do this on a regular basis, the universe will respond and your purpose will start to become clearer… The thoughts that will start coming in will be positive and ones that lead you to your future goals! If there is any advice I can give during this process of finding your purpose and discovering who you really are, it would be to TRUST THE UNIVERSE! The universe will guide you on the right path. As long as you're living a life of gratitude, love and compassion, and keeping your vibration up, the universe will do the rest… Once we connect to our inner selves we become the best we can be.[70]

What are you waiting for to feel your best? The fulfillment that you seek is a choice that you make in the now. No partner or accomplishment or destination is going to create a stable and grounded emotional state that you seek. Those emotional states are found within you, and it is your choice to create them, and you create them first with the mind and activating the desire to feel your best. Everything will shift and transform around you holding on to the notion of how it feels to feel good, to feel your best, to feel confident, to feel secure, to feel safe. What doesn't resonate will come up to be cleared, and you do that with your recognition, and then you drop back into the feelings that you want to feel, these deep emotional grounded states of wellness. However, you feel in the now is what you will carry with you into your future, and your future will respond based on how you feel. So

> you trusting that you're going to feel better when you accomplish a certain thing is an illusion. You're going to feel the same that you feel now. Everything is about the present. So drop in and make the choice to feel your best now, no more waiting.[71]

> Life is truly a balance. Once we master the balance of life, we will start to find true happiness… Find your balance and ask the universe to help you… Balance is also about understanding that, yes, you are a divine being but you are also a human being. You combine these together by connecting with your divine self and by shedding the ego but also having them work together. You're not going to live a life of pure spirit and walk around with a halo on your head. You're still going to face human life issues but you're just going to be able to handle life differently now that you're connected to your divinity. You're basically learning to take your power back… I believe in balance for whatever that may be for you… It is a balance of life on the outside and who you are on the inside… Just like being aware of your thoughts, you need to be aware of your energy. It's a good way to know if you are aligned with your true self as well.[72]

Most of the time before we find our balance and learn how to take our power back, we tend to look for our value and worth in others. We all know the feeling (especially if you identify as a people-pleaser), when we give all our energy away to earn someone's love and affection, only to get rejected in the process,

> It can really hurt when someone doesn't choose you, when they don't show up and leave

> you feeling empty. But here's the beautiful truth in all of it: you have the power to choose yourself. I'm telling you, be there for yourself like nobody else can. Love yourself so fiercely it scares the hell out of anyone who dares doubt you. Because let me remind you, you're an extraordinary soul. You're perfect, flaws and all. And don't get it twisted; I'm not saying this to stroke your ego; self-love is not some cliché or cheesy phrase. It's the realest, most genuine form of love you'll ever know. It's about recognizing your own worth and embracing every damn inch of your journey. It ain't gonna be pretty, it's gonna be messy, raw, and real. But guess what? That's where the magic happens. So my question for you is this: Are you ready to choose yourself?[73]

> It is liberating to realize that you can be happy in this moment for absolutely no reason at all. Simply because it is a choice. And when you realize that, you are no longer dependent on your circumstances to make you happy. Because if we're dependent on our circumstances for our joy and peace in this life, then we're going to remain the victim. It is a choice, and it is a choice that you can make right now, in this moment.[74]

Are you ready to choose yourself? Or are you waiting for someone to choose you first in order to feel loved, happy, and at peace?

> It is no one else's job other than yourself to create your own happiness and your own peace. Someone may have hurt you, did you wrong, abandoned you, weren't there the way you wanted them to be, but if you find yourself saying, "Well, I'm the way I am because of this situation," or

> "I'm the way I am because of this person," you are falling into a very unhealthy cycle of not taking responsibility and not taking charge of your life, your happiness, and your peace. You are the author of your own story, so why not start creating the life that you want today… Start looking within, all of the answers are within. It is our job as adults to create our happiness and our peace. Know that you deserve that. So choose yourself and choose love along the way.[75]

When you do this,

> You are choosing love and openness over insecurity. You are choosing to open up your heart, and to be vulnerable and to share. You're choosing to be really real with yourself. You're choosing to live from a place that feels peaceful to you within you…and because of that you are in alignment with your higher truth, with your higher consciousness, with your higher source. You are in alignment with the divine when you make this choice in any now moment that you choose to make this choice. And this is a continuous effort…or rather attention that you get to give and choose over time, each day, each moment. And you are never stuck if you have chosen, chosen, chosen in a certain direction and wish to change course, wish to change mindset, wish to change how you feel and experience. In any now present moment, you can create any shift that you desire, and in this now present moment you are open, heart open, receiving, allowing, and you may feel that energy flowing through your field, flowing through your body and that is a conscious choice that you have made. And

this is something that you can choose in any moment. This is a tool, this is a skill, and this is an openness that you carry with you.[76]

The truth about every spiritual path is that it guides you home to yourself. Coming home to yourself is a really deep process of reconnection. It is a returning. It is a remembering. Because you move through layers of healing and processing of releasing outdated beliefs that kept you in fragmentation, that kept you in an illusionary limitation…to unwind that corded energy that had you in specific frameworks…to untap unlimited potential, to unblock yourself, unstick yourself, and revive the energetic potential and momentum that is yours. This is spiritual illumination, awakening, enlightenment. It means recalling your energy to yourself, and this happens in layers. There are many layers to you, and where we tend to get stuck right now is in the emotional layer because we have forgotten how to process and release emotions. But emotion has the word motion in it, we are meant to feel and let go… and baggage tends to get stuck. And when we get into a self-relationship, where we develop high level self-awareness, and are able to introspect and observe ourselves, we look at the emotions, we look at the outdated beliefs, we look at where we believe that we are limited and trapped… and in the power of our awareness, we are able to process and thus transform the energy that once bound us in chains to unleash this energy, and allow it once again to rise through us, liberating us to achieve more momentum, to raise your vibration, increasing your energy, increasing your consciousness, enlightening.[77]

When it is all said and done, your main purpose and maybe your only purpose is to live authentically in your truth. You must work to strip away all of the layers of Ego and identity that have been created and strengthened since your early childhood, serving to keep you safe and protect you from further hurt and trauma. In the process, you must be careful not to shed the parts that are authentic to you, and which have been buried under the layers of trauma, shame, and hurt for a long time. You will need to hold space for yourself, be patient, nurture your inner child, and reveal your true Self so that you may live authentically in your truth.

Spiritual Guide Anadasia Rose shares a divine perspective on living authentically,

> You hear people say, “Live authentically in your truth.” But what does that mean exactly? It means showing up as yourself…making space for all emotions, thoughts, and feelings but holding on to none. Being kind and compassionate, but also angry and assertive. Without judgment, without guilt, and without shame. Be confident to say no when you need to and be confident to share love freely, openly, and without attachment. Speak your mind even when your body is on fire because you have been programmed to stay quiet for so long. Tap into the voice that lives within, the creator of all that is, and ask for guidance… as your physical body learns what it is to be free. Use discernment as you learn to trust. And most importantly trust the process. You are unlearning and learning at the same time so if you find yourself to be confused or lost at times, make space for that as well. There is no one and nowhere you need to be other than right here right now in this present moment with yourself. You will find that in time, it will feel more natural, the fire less intense, and something that feels like pas-

> sion instead of fear. You will begin to recognize and embrace yourself as who you truly are, the essence of all that is, the embodiment of divine. And you will love yourself fully as you are, as you have been, and as you will be. So make mistakes. Laugh too hard when the room is silent and speak your mind with a willingness to learn and receive as you give and teach. Listen to your inner child and cater to their needs. Learn from your higher self and honor who you are.[78]

> The end game is to completely come home to yourself, to be consciously connected to every single part of you. That is empowerment. And when you drop into the deepest connection with yourself, it ignites this force, and this force radiates out. And not only do others perceive it subconsciously or in a higher place, but it creates a reaction in you where you literally stop [caring what others think], authentically. And there is nothing more powerful than that, you take care of yourself first, and you only give the overflow, no matter what. You know what you want, and you feel inspired and driven and encouraged to get it because you know your value and you know that you can. And others who don't resonate, there is no attachment. And this neutrality and also supreme belief in yourself will carry you into the fruition and achievement of everything that you want because you are beaming everything that you are.[79]

Section 6.2—Magic Is Real, the Magic Is You!

As we reach the end of our journey through the human-spirit experience together, I encourage you to stay here in this moment, to stay centered in yourself, and centered in Source. Remember, you have everything within you that you need to rewrite your story, to map out your path to wherever you want to go in this lifetime, whether you are ready to head out on your own epic adventure to connect with your next best version of you, or whether you are ready to cultivate peace in your time here in this world.

No matter what path you choose, the choice is yours. There is no wrong choice, you just get a different human-spirit experience. Whether you choose an epic adventure or choose to feel a bit better than you have been, rest in the knowledge that whatever you do is of God, of Source, the Source of everything that exists in the physical world and beyond. God is the Source of the miracles and magic that manifests into wishes, dreams, and opportunities. Have no doubt that the magic is also within you.

Spiritual Guide Brittany Bento emphasizes this point,

> Magic is real. The question is, Do you believe in it? Because when you do, you will realize that magic was within you this entire time. You are magic. The magic in most will remain dormant their entire lives. What most who believe in magic don't realize is that they themselves are the magic. It is not an exterior force. Once you awaken the magic inside of you, you can achieve everything you've ever wanted. It's up to you. You just have to believe, and you don't need anything else but what's within. All you need is yourself, your power, your belief, and your intention. After that, let go and enjoy yourself while you wait for the magic to unfold in front of you. Watch your life play out and don't resist while it's playing to the end. Enjoy it.[80]

Do you believe in Miracles? Do you believe in Magic?

If You Knew How Magic You Really Are[81] by Amanda Rae

If you knew how magic you really are
then when the seas refuse to part
you'd remember you can walk on water
and if you knew how magic you really are
you would howl in the darkness of a new moon night
rather than praying to see the sun
and if you knew how magic you really are
you would kiss the foreheads of everyone who ever tried to make
you feel differently
in gratitude for the opportunity to choose your power
and WHEN you remember how magic you really are
then nothing in existence can stop the creation of the beautiful
life you are sculpting
day by day, heartbeat by heartbeat, breath by breath
just relax and repeat after me, "I am [freaking] magic"

Section 6.3—The Future Is Now!

If I Was the Architect of the Future[82] by Amanda Rae

If I was the architect of the future
I would build bridges where there are canyons
I would build warm hearths to break bread as family,
a safe space to gather in laughter and in tears
to sing ballads of heart songs unsung.
I would build the skylights in dark rooms
so even in the darkest nights of our souls we could still find our
true north.
If I was the artist of the future, I would mold our children with
gentle hands,
and lovingly guide their form as they reveal their shape to me.
I would paint landscapes with untarnished soil

and leave my mark on every canvas I meet.
I would weave together a tapestry of belief systems so large and so rich,
it fortifies the earth in a hug.
If I was the teacher of the future, I would teach little girls that they're the portal to life
and through them creation takes place.
I would help teach young men to protect the tribe and fill their hearts with purpose.
I'd teach the power of our emotions, how to feel and how to flow.
I'd teach the power of our breath and how to use it to grow.
If I was the leader of the future, then I'd lead side by side.
I'd go without in times of drought
and throw celebration when the rain came after.
I'd listen to every comrade. I'd find the common ground,
put the needs of the community above my own desire.
I'd aim to be an example and take responsibility when I fell short.
If I was creating the future then I'd have to embrace my power.
I'd have to let go of my fear of failure and take steps that are empowered.
I'd speak into existence words that uplift and inspire.
I'd blaze a path through darkness for others to follow me there.
I'd realized that the only thing that has power over me is what I will allow
because if I'm creating the future then I'd realize the future is now.

NOTES

Section 1.1—Looking for Peace and Finding Your Self

[1] Breathnach, Sarah, Ban. (1998), Something More: Excavating Your Authentic Self, Grand Central Publishing, p. 49–50.

[2] Breathnach, Sarah, Ban. (1998), Something More: Excavating Your Authentic Self, Grand Central Publishing, p. 41.

[3] Zukav, Gary. (1989), The Seat of the Soul, Fireside: Simon and Schuster, p. 135–139.

[4] Myss, Caroline. (2017), Anatomy of the Spirit: The Seven Stages of Power and Healing, Harmony Books: Penguin Random House LLC, p. xviii - 8.

[5] Curry, April. (2023) Akashic Reader/Teacher and Reiki Master. TikTok video on 2023/06/29.

[6] Myss, Caroline. (2017), Anatomy of the Spirit: The Seven Stages of Power and Healing, Harmony Books: Penguin Random House LLC, p. 257–261.

[7] Breathnach, Sarah, Ban. (1998), Something More: Excavating Your Authentic Self, Grand Central Publishing, p. 15.

Section 2.1—A New Perspective on Health and Evolution

[8] Dispensa, Joe. (2012) Breaking the Habit of Being Yourself: How to Lose Your Mind and Create a New One." Carlsbad, CA: Hay House Inc.

Section 2.2—Relatable Experiences and Keys of Wisdom

[9] American Psychiatric Association. Diagnostic and statistical manual of mental disorders 5ed. (2013) Arlington (VA):

[10] Huntington, Charlie. "People-Pleasing: Definition, Quotes, and Psychology" Berkey Well Being Institute

Section 2.3—The First Step to Growth

[11] Morin, Alain (2011) "Self Awareness Part 1: Definition, Measures, Effects, Functions, and Antecedents" Social and Personality Psychology Compass 5(10:807–823

Section 2.5—The Operating System, Self Concept, and Shadow Work

[12] Dispensa, Joe. (2012) Breaking the Habit of Being Yourself: How to Lose Your Mind and Create a New One." Carlsbad, CA: Hay House Inc.

Section 2.8—Integration and Expansion

[13] Anka, Daryl (2023) Author. TikTok Video 2023/07/02

Section 3.1—Introduction to the Integrated Self Model

[14] Dyer, Wayne. (2006), Being in balance: 9 principles for creating habits to match your desires, Hay House, p. xi.

[15] Dyer, Wayne. (2006), Being in balance: 9 principles for creating habits to match your desires, Hay House, p. xi.

Section 3.5—Balance of Ego-Soul Growth

[16] Maslow, Abraham H. (1962, 20011). Towards a Psychology of Being, Martino Publishing, p.181.

[17] Bento, Brittany. (2023) Spiritual Teacher and Medium. TikTok video on 2023/01/22.

Section 3.7—Influence of Maslow's Hierarchy of Needs

[18] Maslow, Abraham H. (1943, 2013). "A theory of human motivation." Psychological Review, Martino Publishing, 50 (4): 370–396, p.14.

[19] Kaufman, Scott Barry, Ph.D. (2020). Transcend: The new science of self-actualization, TarcherPerigee: Penguin Random House LLC, p. xxx.

[20] Maslow, Abraham H. (1962, 20011). Towards a Psychology of Being, Martino Publishing, p.25.

[21] Kaufman, Scott Barry, Ph.D. (2020). Transcend: The new science of self-actualization, TarcherPerigee: Penguin Random House LLC, p. xxx.

[22] Kaufman, Scott Barry, Ph.D. (2020). Transcend: The new science of self-actualization, TarcherPerigee: Penguin Random House LLC, p. xxxi.

[23] Maslow, Abraham H. (1962, 20011). Towards a Psychology of Being, Martino Publishing, p. 23.

[24] Smith, Landon, T. (2017). Meet Maslow, Make Profits Easy LLC, p. 7.

[25] Smith, Landon, T. (2017). Meet Maslow, Make Profits Easy LLC, p. 10.

[26] Maslow, Abraham H. (1962, 20011). Towards a Psychology of Being, Martino Publishing, p. 67.

[27] Maslow, Abraham H. (1962, 20011). Towards a Psychology of Being, Martino Publishing, p. 91.

[28] Maslow, Abraham H. (1962, 20011). Towards a Psychology of Being, Martino Publishing, p.198.

Section 3.8—Purpose of the Human-Spirit Experience

[29] Liberatore, Anna. (2022) Inspirational Writer. TikTok video 2022/12/07: Excerpt from book: "Your Soul's Blueprint."

[30] Bento, Brittany. (2023) Spiritual Teacher and Medium. TikTok video 2023/02/16.

[31] Smith, Landon, T. (2017). Meet Maslow, Make Profits Easy LLC, p. 99.

Section 4.1—Initiation of Human-Spirit Experience

[32] Walsch, Neale Donald. (1995), Conversations with God Book 1, G.P. Putnam's Sons, New York, New York, p. 24–27.

Section 5.1—The Steps Toward Balance and Growth

[33] Singer, Michael A. (2007), the untethered soul: the journey beyond yourself, New Harbinger Publications, Inc. p. 27.

[34] Gingrich, Tiffany. (2023) Transformational Mindset Coach. TikTok video 2023/03/21 / 2023/03/29 / 2023/5-05.

[35] Singer, Michael A. (2007), the untethered soul: the journey beyond yourself, New Harbinger Publications, Inc. p. 95.

Section 5.2—Understand and Document Your Personal Story

[36] Keirsey, David / Bates, Marilyn. (1984), Please Understand Me: Character and Temperament Types, Gnosology Books Ltd.

Section 5.6—Assess Current State of Ego Development

[37] Bradshaw, John. (1988, 2005), Healing the Shame that Binds You, Health Communications, Inc.

[38] Bradshaw, John. (1992), Creating Love: The Next Great Stage of Growth, Bantam Books.

[39] Ruiz, Don Miguel. (1997), The Four Agreements, Amber-Allen Publishing.

[40] Hendricks, Gay / Hendricks, Kathlyn. (1990), Conscious Loving: The Journey to Co-Commitment, Bantam Books.

[41] Hargis, Jennifer. (2023) Spiritual Coach. TikTok video 2023/05/13.

[42] Singer, Michael A. (2007), the untethered soul: the journey beyond yourself, New Harbinger Publications, Inc. p. 10.

Section 5.7—Assess Current State of Soul Evolution

[43] Redfield, James. (1993), The Celestine Prophecy: An Adventure, Warner Books.

[44] Ruiz, Don Miguel. (1997), The Four Agreements, Amber-Allen Publishing, Inc.

[45] Walsch, Neale Donald. (1995), Conversations with God Book 1, G.P. Putnam's Sons, New York, New York.

[46] Dyer, Wayne W. (2004), The Power of Intention: Learning to Co-create Your World Your Way, Hay House.

[47] Chopra, Deepak. (1994), The Seven Spiritual Laws of Success: A Practical Guide to the Fulfillment of Your Dreams, New World Library.

[48] Hargis, Jennifer. (2023) Spiritual Coach. TikTok video 2023/02/26.

Section 5.8—Assess your Level of Consciousness

[49] Hawkins, David, R. (2002), Power vs. force: The hidden determinants of human behavior, Hay House, p. 9–24.

[50] Hawkins, David, R. (2002), Power vs. force: The hidden determinants of human behavior, Hay House, p. 76.

[51] Hawkins, David, R. (2002), Power vs. force: The hidden determinants of human behavior, Hay House, p. 67.

[52] Hawkins, David, R. (2002), Power vs. force: The hidden determinants of human behavior, Hay House, p. 68–69.

[53] Hawkins, David, R. (2002), Power vs. force: The hidden determinants of human behavior, Hay House, p. 75–94.

Section 5.9—Assess Personal Ego Identity

[54] Keirsey, David, / Bates, Marilyn. (1984). Please Understand Me: Character and Temperament, Gnosology Books Ltd.

[55] Briggs-Myers, Isabel / Myers, Peter B. (1980, 1995). Gifts Differing: Understanding Personality Type, CPP, Inc / Davies Black Publishing.

[56] Keirsey, David / Bates, Marilyn. (1984). Please Understand Me: Character and Temperament, Gnosology Books Ltd., p. 189–192.

[57] Keirsey, David / Bates, Marilyn. (1984). Please Understand Me: Character and Temperament, Gnosology Books Ltd., p. 170–172.

[58] Thomas, Adri. (2023) Life Coach. TikTok video 2023/04/18.

[59] Gingrich, Tiffany. (2023) Transformational Mindset Coach. TikTok video 2023/04/06.

[60] Chopra, Deepak. (1994), The Seven Spiritual Laws of Success: A Practical Guide to the Fulfillment of Your Dreams, New World Library. p. 40–41.

[61] Gingrich, Tiffany. (2023) Transformational Mindset Coach. TikTok video 2023/04/21.

[62] Nicole, Melissa. (2023) Life and Mindset Coach. TikTok video 2023/05/21.

Section 5.11—Achieving Balance and Integration

[63] Goddard, Neville. (2012), The Neville Goddard Deluxe Collection: The Power of Awareness, Noah Press. p. 383.

[64] Saint Claire, Stephanie. (2023) The Inner Child Whisperer, Life Coach. TikTok video 2023/04/21.

[65] Saint Claire, Stephanie. (2023) The Inner Child Whisperer, Life Coach. TikTok video 2023/04/08.

[66] Tolle, Eckhart. (1999), The Power of Now: A Guide to Spiritual Enlightenment, New World Library. p. 46.

[67] Gingrich, Tiffany. (2023) Transformational Mindset Coach. TikTok video 2022/08/21.

Section 6.1—Now that you know your story, what are you going to do?

[68] Curry, April. (2023) Akashic Reader-Teacher and Reiki Master. TikTok video on 2023/06/25.

[69] Goicoechea, Samantha. (2023). TikTok video on 2023/06/29.

[70] Barnett, Kira. (2021), Finding Your Destiny and Your Reason for Existing: The Inner Map, Self-published, Chapter 12: Finding your purpose, just follow the Inner Map.

[71] Kavara, Kali. (2023), Ascension Guide and Light Healer. TikTok video 2023/05/18.

[72] Barnett, Kira. (2021), Finding Your Destiny and Your Reason for Existing: The Inner Map, Self-published, Chapter 8: The Balance of Life.

[73] Rener, Hannah. (2023) Creative, Heart-Centered Influencer. TikTok video 2023/07/12.

[74] Gingrich, Tiffany. (2023) Transformational Mindset Coach. TikTok video 2023/08/08.

[75] Nicole, Melissa. (2023) Life and Mindset Coach. TikTok video 2023/06/30.

[76] Angela Eleni. (2023) Spiritual Advisor. TikTok video 2023/06/30.

[77] Kavara, Kali. (2023), Ascension Guide and Light Healer. TikTok video 2023/07/10.

[78] Anadasia Rose. (2023) Spiritual Guide. TikTok video 2023/06/23.

[79] Kavara, Kali. (2023), Ascension Guide and Light Healer. TikTok video 2023/07/04.

Section 6.2—In the end, the magic is real —the magic is YOU!

[80] Bento, Brittany. (2023) Spiritual Teacher and Medium. TikTok video 2023/05/06.

[81] Rae, Amanda. (2023) If You Knew How Magic You Really Are. Life Coach. TikTok video 2023/02/26.

Section 6.3—Time to Create Your Future… The Future is Now!

[82] Rae, Amanda. (2023) If I was the Architect of the Future, Life Coach. TikTok video 2023/02/24.

Addendum: The Integrated Self Model – Full Set of Images (See Page 56)

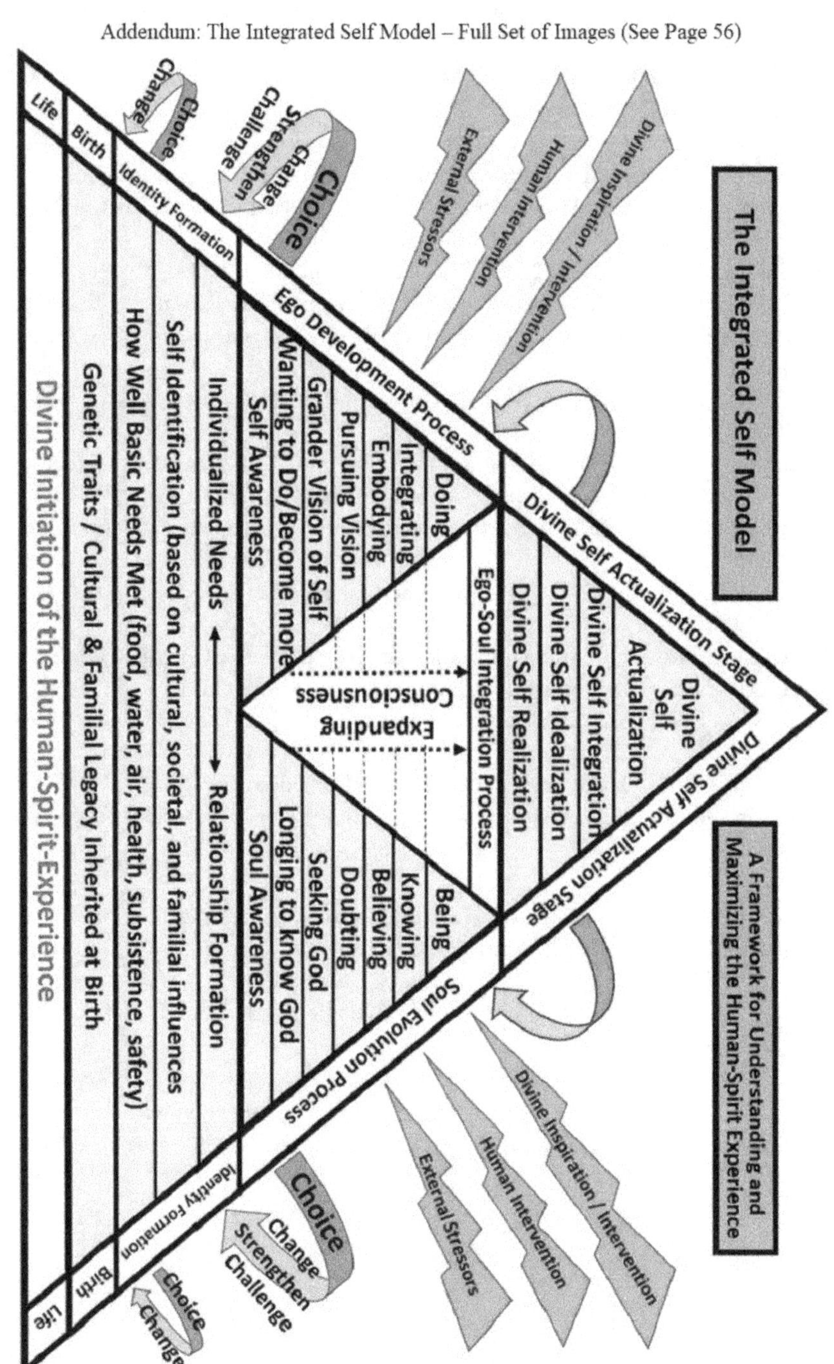

Addendum: The Integrated Self Model – Full Set of Images (See Page 91)

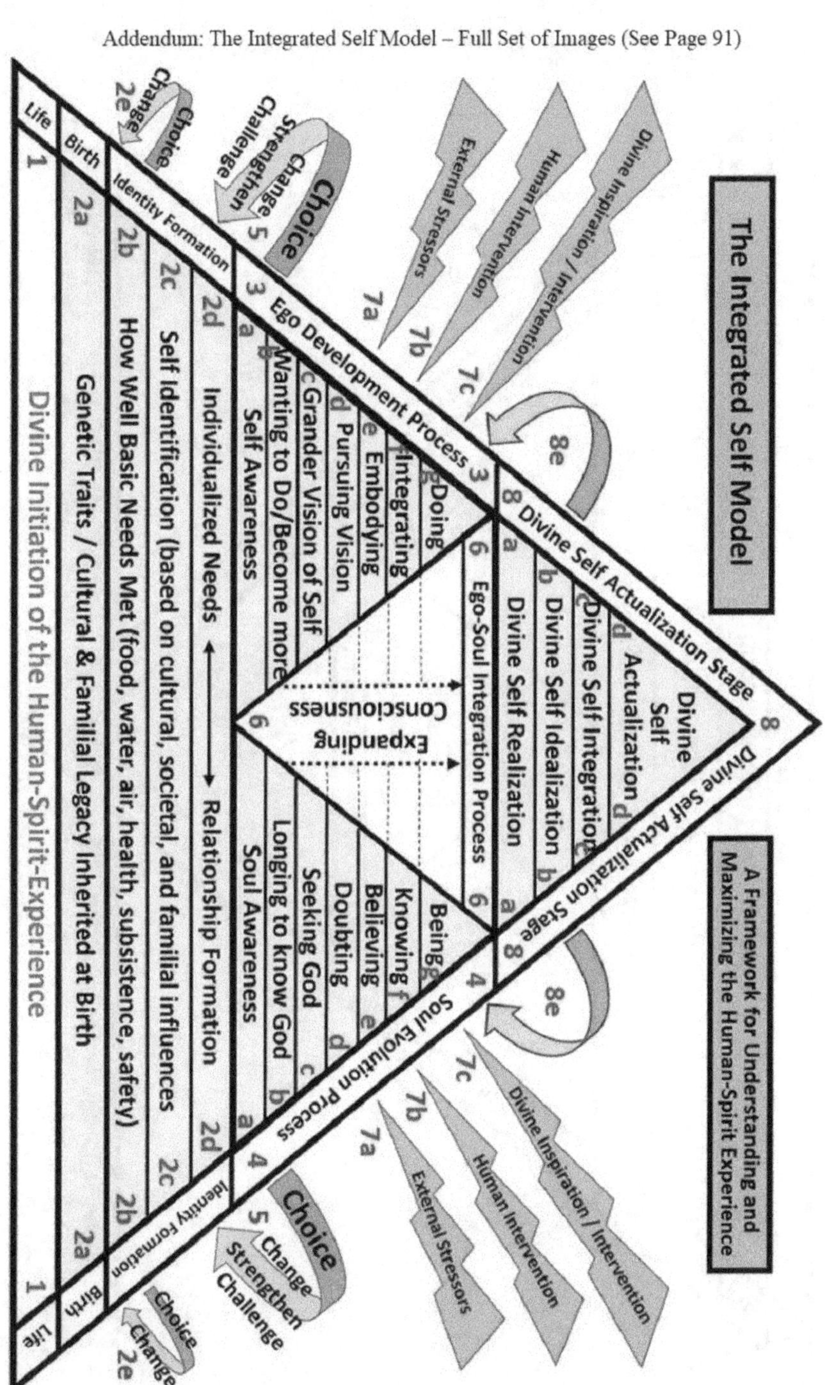

Addendum: The Integrated Self Model – Full Set of Images (See Page 58)

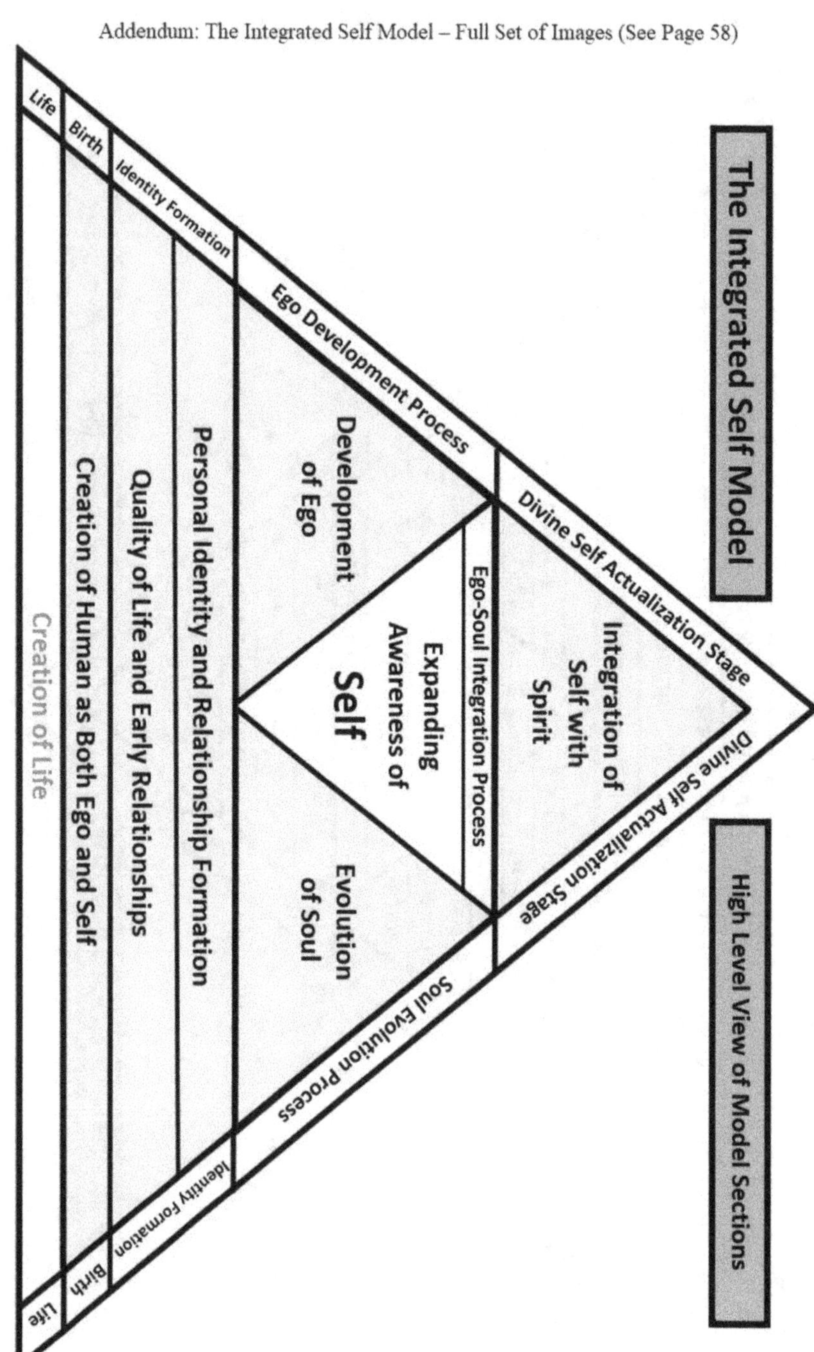

Addendum: The Integrated Self Model – Full Set of Images (See Page 58)

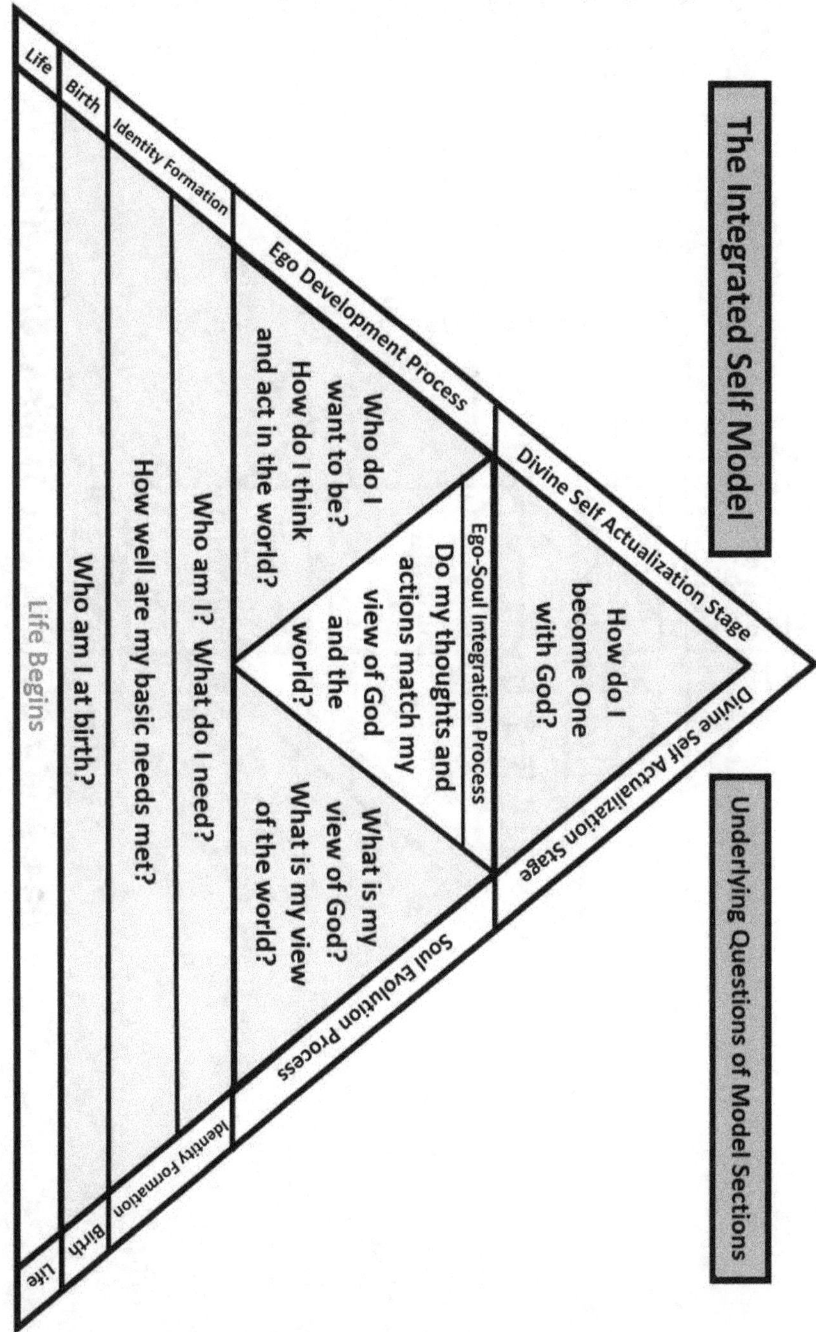

Addendum: The Integrated Self Model – Full Set of Images (See Page 67)

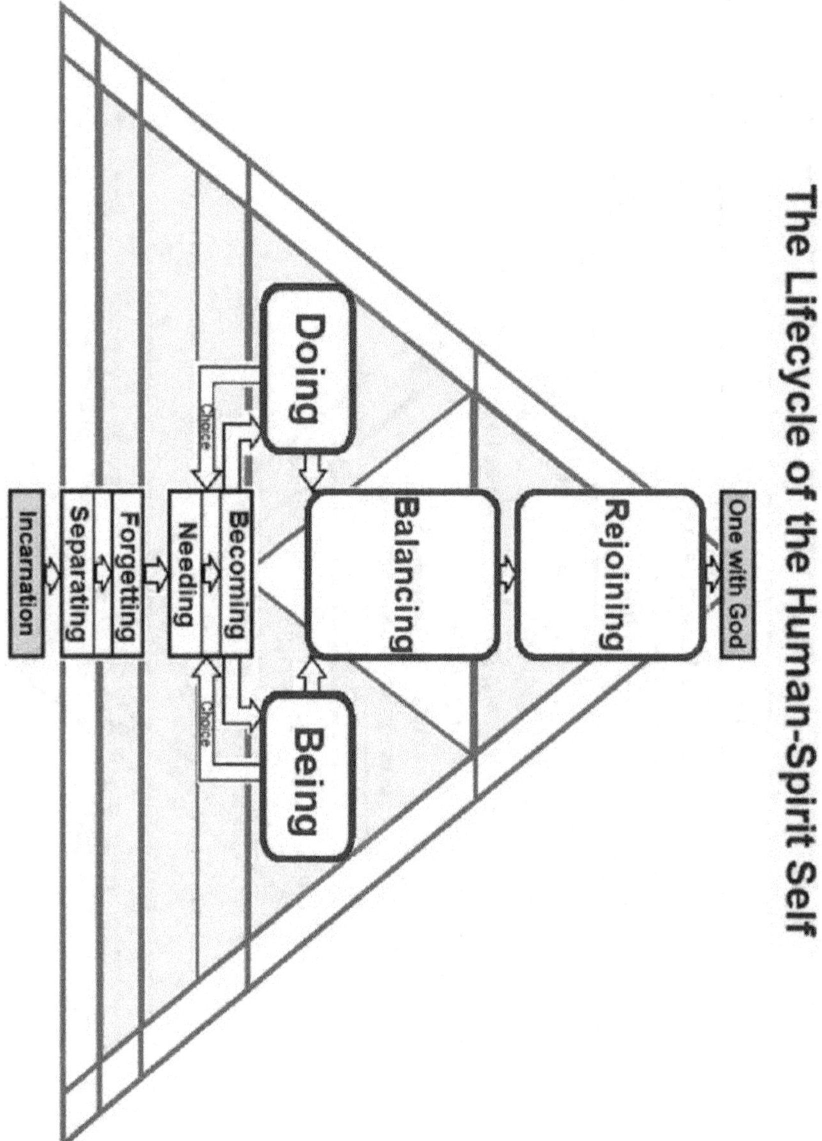

Addendum: The Integrated Self Model – Full Set of Images (See Page 67)

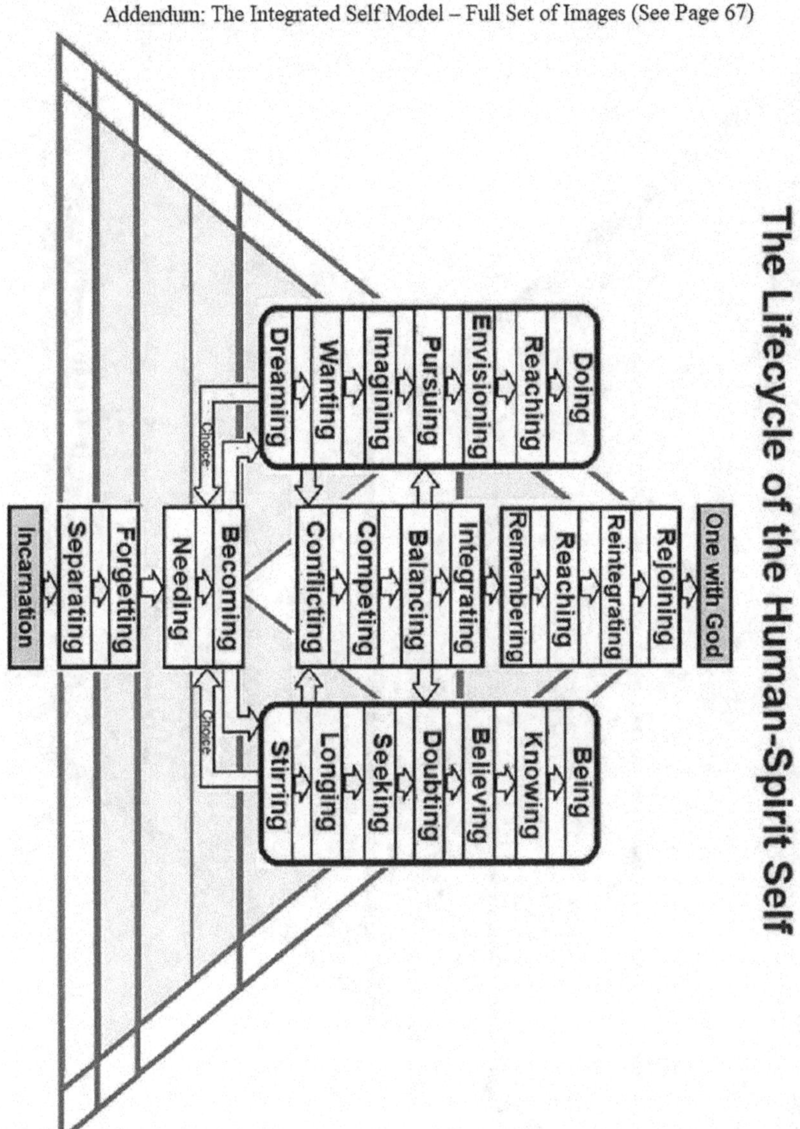

Addendum: The Integrated Self Model – Full Set of Images (See Page 84)

Maslow's Hierarchy of Needs

Self Actualization

Self Esteem

Longing & Belonging

Safety

Physiological

Addendum: The Integrated Self Model – Full Set of Images (See Page 84)

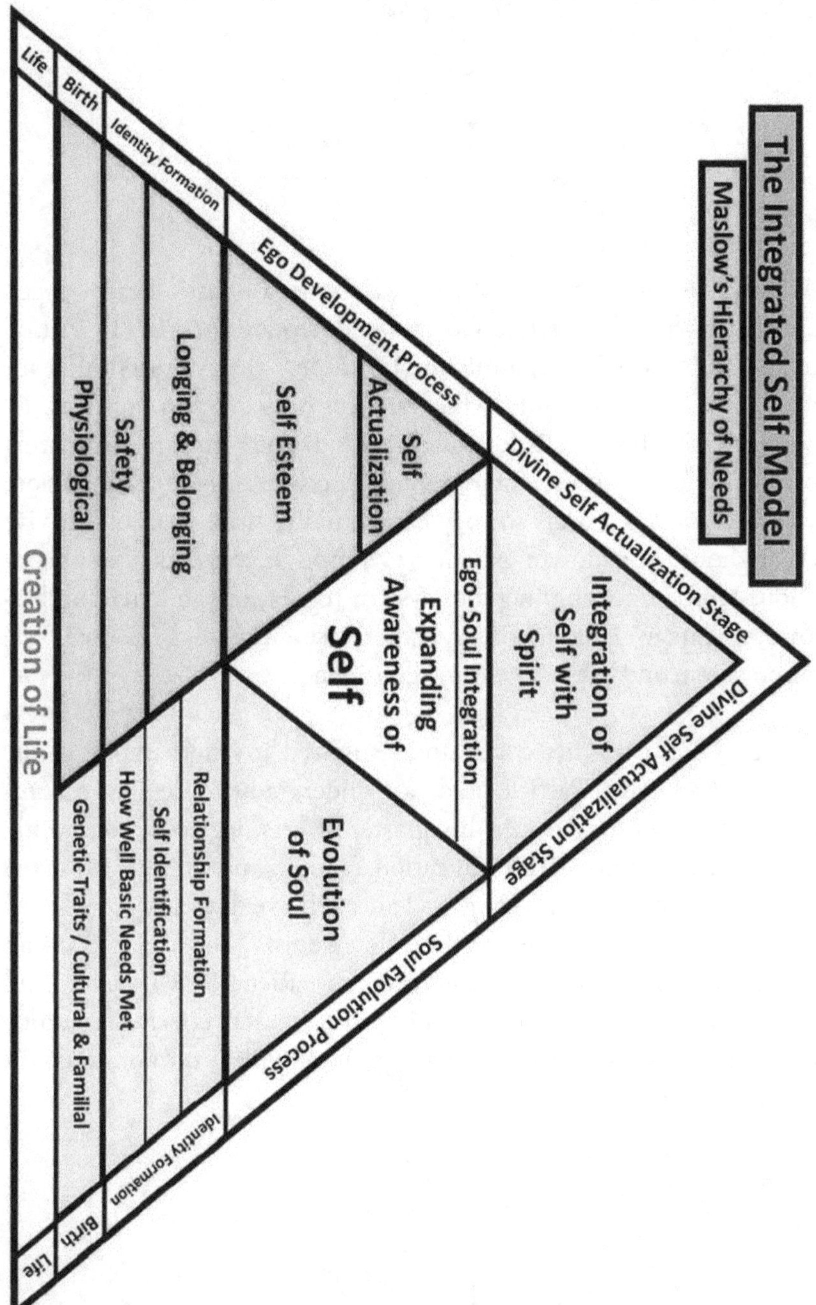

ABOUT THE AUTHORS

Arianna Sidway is currently a board-certified holistic health coach continuing her education to receive her doctorate and PhD in natural medicine. Arianna is on a mission to support the evolution of beautiful souls from the inside, which reflects outwardly in our lives. By coaching clients on holistic health of mind, body, and spirit, Arianna connects her clients to their personal power, authentic expression, and abundant mindsets so they can actually thrive, not just survive throughout their human experience. Through concepts like subconscious reprogramming, nervous system regulation, and creating balance, clients are able to finally experience emotional freedom, feel empowered, and express genuine confidence.

Patrick Diorio is a life coach and registered psychotherapist in the state of Colorado. Patrick holds an undergraduate degree in communication and has earned his master of arts degree in counseling psychology and counselor education (couple and family) from the University of Colorado Denver. Patrick has experience as a street counselor serving the Denver homeless youths (under eighteen), an internship counselor in an intensive outpatient (IOP) center, and a registered psychotherapist in his private practice, serving adults, teens, and children in individual, group, couple, and family counseling sessions.

Printed in the USA
CPSIA information can be obtained
at www.ICGtesting.com
LVHW010136100824
787870LV00001B/11